In the Shadow of My Brother's Cold Blood

As told to Linda LeBert-Corbello, PhD by David Hickock

iUniverse, Inc.
New York   Bloomington

iUniverse books may be ordered through booksellers or by contacting:

iUniverse
1663 Liberty Drive
Bloomington, IN 47403
www.iuniverse.com
1-800-Authors (1-800-288-4677)

Because of the dynamic nature of the Internet, any Web addresses or links contained in this book may have changed since publication and may no longer be valid. The views expressed in this work are solely those of the author and do not necessarily reflect the views of the publisher, and the publisher hereby disclaims any responsibility for them.

ISBN: 978-1-4502-1515-2 (sc)
ISBN: 978-1-4502-1513-8 (hc)
ISBN: 978-1-4502-1514-5 (ebook)

Library of Congress Control Number: 2010902654

Printed in the United States of America

iUniverse rev. date: 03/29/2010

Dedicated to those who believed................

*Diana, my cousin, my sister, my friend, who
excitedly asked for the first copy of this book...*

*Bob, my first love, who believed until
the end that I could do anything...*

*Dave, for sharing his story so others could
learn from his life experiences...*

I miss each of you so much.

Preface

My name is Dave and I am a murderer. I never pulled the trigger of a gun or held a knife to kill another person, but I am imprisoned because of my brother's actions. Yes, and as in all cases of this sort, I can truthfully say that my personal trial was unfair. I was unjustly convicted by society's judgment and my own fears, and I have spent a lifetime desperately crying out for true justice. This devastating chain of events began in the year 1959, just months after one tragic night changed my life. My trial was never in a courtroom. The opportunity to prove my innocence was never provided. My sentence was never published in the newspapers. However, I was forced to endure a lifetime of fear, cowardly running, immense sadness, and pain.

One may think I am just an old man rambling on about something of which I know nothing. But I know about murder, about trials, and about the aftermath of such things. I know about the injustice of being associated with a murder I did not commit. I was not present the night of the horrific murders of 1959. I never ventured to Holcomb, Kansas. I had never heard of the Clutter family. Yet, it was I who ran fearfully for a lifetime to erase the pain and the torment of being accused of murder by society.

Do I want to relive the pain? Not necessarily! I do want to determine just exactly how and why the lives of two Kansas families merged on one solemn night never to be separated again. The names

Hickock and Clutter became known across the entire United States, and Truman Capote eventually told the story of the Clutter murders in his classic book *In Cold Blood*.

I am Walter David Hickock. This story is definitely my story, but it would not exist without two convicted murderers: Richard Eugene Hickock and Perry Edward Smith. They actually lived this story. They were the actors on a stage that created the intense drama that would be reviled by the nation. As much as the American people hated and feared the men and decried the murders, nearly everyone, it seemed, wanted to know every sordid detail. I was one of their victims. In just one night, my life was ruined. People treated me as though I, too, was a murderer. I was never to be the same again. In fact, the lives of my mom and dad were also ruined on that night. My parents rapidly became empty shells of the people they were prior to November 15, 1959.

My account is both the same and starkly different from Capote's. Capote was an author and later noted as one of the greatest in America. He did use many of the details of the crime in his book. He interviewed everyone he possibly could to obtain the facts. He became emotionally charged as he spent copious amounts of time with Richard Eugene Hickock and Perry Edward Smith. Finally, after years of intensive work, he published a book that continues to be read all these years later. Capote gave an account of a horrific murder by intertwining the facts of the murder with a bit of his own conjectures on the events and the people involved.

My account is also emotionally charged, but with different emotions. My story is more personal because it involves my own incredible grief and great denial. I heard the facts as Capote did, but I wanted to believe something else. I refused to speak to anyone about the crime. I tried to ignore people's stares, their questions, and the repulsive looks on their faces when they saw me … a Hickock.

Grief is an emotional response to tragic situations that are beyond our control. I have learned that the stages of grief can haunt one for a lifetime. I especially held tight-fistedly to the denial stage. Even though there were times when I knew deep down inside that Dick was guilty of murder, my broken heart and my love for my brother made me deny the reality. I could not readily admit that Dick was guilty. Yet, all evidence pointed otherwise. I so wanted Dick to be innocent. That denial became my personal friend. While Capote had objectivity, my love for my brother blocked my objectivity. I lived a lifetime with an aching, broken heart feeding the denial that my brother was in fact a cold-blooded killer! I often wondered how my brother Dick could possibly have murdered four innocent people in a town across the state of Kansas from where we lived. He was my brother, after all, my older brother.

For by grace are ye saved through faith; and that not of yourselves: it is the gift of God.

The Open Bible, 1975, p. 1106

Introduction

I met the brother of a murderer. His name was Dave. He sauntered into my office in a desperate and humble search to find an author to write his tragic story. Once Dave began talking, I was riveted. It was not merely the fact that he was associated with one of America's most brutal and infamous murders. It was not just that he was a sad, confused man. I could clearly see that underneath all the layers of sadness and pain he possessed a gentle spirit wounded by the hurtful experiences of a lifetime. Within Walter David Hickock's words, and deeply rooted in his pain, there was a story that needed to be heard by all. Grace had indeed brought him to me, and I had to become part of his suffering to see that gift of grace working in his life.

Human suffering comes into all of our lives, but do we understand the role it plays in determining who we become? Dave's request was simple and very straightforward. He wanted the world to know "the other side of the story." How grateful I am that I took the time to listen to his urgent plea. Dave's message was grounded in the sincerity of a man who had experienced the most difficult of times, difficulties that involved more notoriety for a country boy than can ever be imagined! The crime was just the beginning of a lifetime of fear, doubt, and complete isolation.

Dave wanted the world to know, but the more important reason for sharing his story was that he desperately wanted his children to know of his realization during the twilight years of his life that he knew they had also suffered greatly in their association with a murderer. The true murderer was not Dave; it was Dave's brother, Richard Eugene Hickock. Dave was only guilty of being the brother of a cold-blooded killer. Dave's regrets were many. Dave wanted to tell the story of his deeply rooted regret for being a coward who ran away from the reality and pain of murder. He realized that in running he gave up on every person he cared about or loved. His neglect left a wall between him and his children. He longed to deal with all aspects of what had happened, put it into perspective, and, finally, as a man in his late sixties, move on with his life without the heavy burden he had carried for so long.

Dave was in his early twenties when he was thrown into a world of which he knew nothing about. Nothing could have prepared him for the fear he experienced as he faced cold jails, imposing prisons, and half-truths. His inner skills at this vulnerable age were inappropriate to the situation in which he found himself. Dave did not know how to tap into outside resources that could have possibly counseled him in the grieving process. Thus, he did the only thing he knew how to do: run, and run for a lifetime he did. His journey through the stages of grief lasted almost fifty years and took him through various places in the United States.

He had hopes that his story would be of assistance to others who have had similar life-changing events in their lives. Through his tear-filled eyes, I saw a depth of pain that was brimming with an urgency to be shared. I knew I wanted to be part of his efforts to share his story. His longing became my longing. More importantly, I wanted to assist Dave in using his story as a mechanism to release him from the prison and confining bondage of his sad memories.

I learned much about Dave during our first formal meeting. The kindness of his blue eyes did not fully reveal the torment that haunted his mind and soul. We met for weekly sessions for about eighteen months. In these sessions, Dave would painfully and tearfully tell of his encounter with evil. Each time we met I would be the listener. As he spoke of his experiences in life, I often asked questions to make sure I understood everything he was trying to convey. I knew that I had to establish who he really was as a person. He was so much more than the coward he believed himself to be. I also knew the importance of determining how the Hickock family lived. After all, a murderer in your midst has to generate evil in a household, does it not? Were there any signs to warn members of the family of the evil that was to enter their placid lives?

I was amazed as Dave, a kind and gentle man, answered my questions. He gave insight into astonishing facts that were born of simplistic surroundings. Each week we would talk and I would take notes, rushing home to write yet another chapter. Dave gave me the details I needed to recreate his story, some of which I include as dialogue in this book, reflecting as best as possible Dave's memories of what happened. Every week when we met in Dave's home, I read what I had written. At times, he corrected me or added more information that he had remembered from my previous visit. At other times, he shared news articles, photographs, or handwritten notes.

One of the most dramatic and emotional visits occurred after many sessions and the sharing of many articles I had found on the crime when I finally said, "Dave, can you honestly tell me that your brother was in any way innocent of this crime after all we have read and discussed?" Dave rested his head on the table and cried. After a while, he looked up and said, "No, I guess I cannot say that." That was one of the moments in which I thought maybe this was the whole reason he found me. He finally had someone to listen and help him figure out the many reasons he ran for a lifetime and kept at bay any remembrances of the crimes. He could finally say aloud to someone … *My brother is guilty.*

On another afternoon, when I read him the chapter that dealt with his recollections of the day he and his father went to Garden City, Kansas, to visit his brother after he was arrested for the murders, Dave sat stunned with teary eyes and said, "Linda, it was like you were there with me and my dad." I cried at that moment because I had captured his sorrow, fear, and grief in words. That was when I just knew we had to get all the details he could possibly remember into his story.

It became apparent that Dave needed to understand his story, but he needed the assistance of all others that participated in the tragedy to help him fully comprehend the implications and consequences of the events. Thus, I was privileged to communicate with Carol, Dick Hickock's first wife, and Les, Dick's friend and minister who was with Dick the evening he was hung from the gallows. The weekly sessions I shared with Dave brought me into a world of which I had no knowledge. There were times as I took notes that I was frightened, and at other times I was in disbelief. Yet, I wanted to know everything I could about Dave, the Hickocks, and the tragedy.

When the initial manuscript was almost complete, my husband Bob of thirty-seven years died of a massive heart attack. I was frozen in my own grief with so many new adjustments; I could not continue with the work on the manuscript. However, the summer following Bob's death I did go to Florida to have a friend, Cindy Ladkani, an outstanding English teacher, work with me on the manuscript. Upon returning to Louisiana I once again could not touch the manuscript. Depression was the most probable factor, but I just could not concentrate. The ability to write had abandoned me. Even my personal journals were just filled with rambled words, thoughts, and emotions … all indicative of my own grief and depression.

As the months continued to move on, I was haunted by my inability to finish the work I had begun for Dave. Dave would periodically come by my office to see if I had continued. Patiently, he would inquire of my progress toward publication of the book. I promised him I would finish. I held and studied photos from his family album. I read scriptures found in Dave's mom's wallet. I reread notes that Dave had written to me, thoughts he had during the week that he saved to share with me on those weekly visits. I wondered how I could make the world know of Dave's considerable burden. I would often look at these pieces of a family's life and wonder how and what I was to do with it all. I was the only person in the world to know the intimate details of Dave's story.

As a part of my healing process, I left on a pilgrimage to Europe to visit shrines at Fatima, Portugal, and Lourdes, France, seeking peace and a balance to my life that had literally changed in one afternoon with the death of a husband I had known since I was sixteen years old. Upon my return on June 26, 2008, I was informed that Walter David "Dave" Hickock had died on June 24, 2008. To add to this fact was the incredibly shocking news that Dave had died on Bob's birthday. Was that some sort of sign or was it merely a coincidence? I struggled again with the fact that I had not completed this project during Dave's lifetime. Guilt has a crippling hold. I was once again frozen with a loss that was unexplainable. You see, I had come to love Dave in a maternal way. I wanted to help "save" him from himself.

The project languished until I married Gregory, who gently prodded me to continue on with the work on this book. He fully understood the burden I carried with Dave's message and my challenge to share it. As I sit and write the final words, I am grateful to have had the privilege of these three men in my life. My deceased husband Bob, Dave, and now my new husband Gregory. They all share in the success of the completion of this project. Each believed that I could write this book. Each gave me courage that even with copious words I cannot define. I am just grateful for the grace that allowed three lives to cross my path to believe in and encourage me.

PART 1
Richard Eugene Hickock

Chapter One
A Most Vile Murder

On that dreadful November 14, 1959, a Saturday, Dick informed my parents that he was going with a friend to assist him in finding his sister in Fort Scott. He casually mentioned that his return would be very late. My parents had no reason to doubt that he was going to do exactly that. Dick drove to the bus station in Kansas City and picked up Perry Smith, a prison buddy who had also recently been released from prison. They drove to Emporia, Kansas, and while there visited a variety store to select items they believed they needed for the evening's adventure.

What strange items they purchased for such a supposedly innocent trip! My brother and his friend purchased rubber gloves and a large amount of white nylon cord. They wanted to obtain black stockings to wear over their heads to make sure that they could not be identified, but decided against it because obtaining them proved to be problematic. These initial items would be utilized in a murder of four innocent people in a town across the state of Kansas by midnight.

After the arrests on December 30, 1959, Dick was very straightforward about the murders when Dad and I went to see him. He spoke about the crime in detail at the Garden City County Jail. The first statements Dick said to me regarding the murders were contradictory. His first words to Dad and me are embedded in my

1

mind. He emphatically told us that all they had planned to do was rob the Clutter home. Yet, before he began his story I knew Dick had taken a gun with him and that he had invited a known killer to accompany him on his adventure.

He told us this: "*I just wanted to rob that house. You just gotta believe me. An inmate from the prison told me that this Clutter guy in Holcomb had a safe in his house with a large amount of money in it, thousands and thousands of dollars. I brought the gun in case there were problems. I asked Perry Smith to come along because I knew he would pull the trigger if we needed to. Perry had told me he had killed before. Perry liked the idea of the money because he had some wild dreams of what he was going to do to spend the money.*"

Dick also stated to me more than once, "*Dave, I don't know how it all changed so fast. I just wanted to rob the place. Perry actually threatened me. He just went crazy. I thought he would kill me too.*" These many years later I have come to realize I was listening to the words of a sociopath. The characteristic nature of a sociopath is that he can justify his irrational behavior with convincing words. I wanted to believe his words; that was the only hope I had left.

As I sat in the visiting area of the jail and listened to my brother's contradictory words and jumbled thoughts, I found it difficult to make any sense of what he was saying. I told Dick to slow down and go back slowly over the events of the night. I just did not want to believe my brother could possibly plan such an ordeal. He drew a deep breath and told me the following story, a story that should have erased all doubt.

"*We drove to the Clutter home and did not even have to break in. The door was open and we just walked in. At first, I thought it was going to be an easy score just as I had planned. All I figured we had to do was find the safe, take the money, and get out of there. We would not need rope to tie anyone up after all. The problem was that we could not find a safe. We went searching through the house to find the Clutter man. After seeing Mr. Clutter for the first time, I felt a little bad. He was just an ordinary man. He was bent on not telling us where the safe was and he even offered to write us a check. Can you believe that guy, Dave? Write us a check! Once inside the Clutter home and being so frustrated because we could not find a safe, we tied up all members of the family. We tied the mother and daughter in their bedrooms. We took Mr. Clutter and the boy down to the basement and tied them up. Perry was especially good at tying the knots so the Clutters could not undo them. We taped their mouths so no one could scream."*

As Dick told me his version of the evening's events my body became frozen with fear. All I could think about was the description I had in my mind about Herb Clutter. According to what the news reports said, this man was, as Dick commented, an ordinary man. He was like most men in that he worked hard and was raising a family in a decent manner. He was extraordinary, as we soon discovered, in that he was widely respected in the Holcomb community. He was a prominent member of the First Methodist Church. He was well known in the field of agriculture and served as a member of some kind of farm board. It seemed that everyone really respected Herb Clutter. Man, I kept thinking, why would anyone want to murder such a nice guy? As Dick talked about that night, I began to realize that my brother might just be a killer. My brother was definitely a part of the most horrendous crime of our day.

Dick continued his story by laying the blame on Perry Smith. He said: *"Dave, Perry had used a knife to slash Mr. Clutter's neck. He told me to finish the job. I told him, 'Man, I am not doing that to that old man!' Perry went berserk and screamed, 'If you do not finish the job on the old man's neck, you will be next to have your neck slashed.' I was afraid not to listen to him."*

Dick stated that he complied with the request, but mentioned that he was sure that Mr. Clutter was already dead. As I sat listening to Dick talk, I knew there was something totally insane about this story, but I could not pinpoint what it was. This was my brother was all I could think. I didn't know then that his words portrayed a sociopath's manner of thinking. He actually believed in his own innocence as he related the events of the evening.

In all the descriptions of the brutality of the shootings and the use of the knife to slash Mr. Clutter's neck, Dick claimed his innocence to me and to my parents until the very day he was to hang for his crimes. I wanted to believe him, but I knew deep down that he wasn't a reliable source of information. Dick promised us that he had nothing to do with the actual slayings. However, my family and I came to understand that Dick had masterminded the evil that ensued on November 15, 1959.

My brother had offered an invitation to Perry Smith to join him in what he called a robbery. He had placed a gun in the family car and was the driver of that car to the murder scene. By no means was my brother innocent or less guilty than Perry Smith. He was not just an accomplice. I now know that he was guilty … just plain guilty. It has taken me all these years to look this monstrous ordeal in the face, and to try to decode all of the messages and decipher where reality and fantasy collide.

When I recount Dick's chilling conclusion to this tale, and even then as I listened to the information that Dick shared, I wondered who this man was that proceeded to share such sordid details. Could he really be my brother? Dick stated that in the brief moments after using the knife on Mr. Clutter, he told Perry that he would like to rape the Clutter daughter. Perry became very upset. In fact, Dick said that he thought that simple remark pushed Perry Smith over the edge. Dick explained that it was at this point that Smith went to the couch in the basement and shot the Clutter son and the father. He ran up the basement stairs, gun in hand, and began fatally shooting the other members of the Clutter family.

Dick told me without any shame of his cowardice. *"Dave, I was afraid at that time that Perry was going to kill me, too. I didn't touch the Clutter daughter. After Perry shot everyone, we left, taking less than fifty dollars, a transistor radio, and a pair of binoculars from the Clutter family home. Man, were we feeling let down. We thought we were going to make a big score by robbing Clutter's safe."* I could not believe what I was hearing. My brother was worried about "a big score" when he had just participated in the murder of four people.

I remember sitting in that jail and hearing those words and feeling stunned into disbelief. This was my brother. How in the world could he have been with such a weirdo, someone so violently dangerous? Then I would spend a moment or two thinking that maybe Dick was the weirdo. I sat in that jail thinking that my parents had made comments about Perry Smith before the murders. They had met him in a brief encounter and had commented that they did not think he was a good influence on Dick. They thought Perry had a strange way about him. He was just not a likeable guy. At least, this is how my parents perceived him.

Personally, I never met Perry. I did see him later in prison shortly before the execution when visiting my brother. He made a waving motion with his hand to me, but even then I knew there was something strangely sad and evil about him. I wondered if others felt the same way about Dick. I deeply wanted to blame everything that happened on Perry Smith, and because of this, I spent many years in denial.

As I tell this story, it breaks my heart to look this evil in the eye and admit that my brother was the mastermind, the catalyst, and a murderer in this horrifying chain of events. I doubt that there was much truth in the stories my brother told me, but there was much evidence that he was deranged. His justifications were only fragments of the harsh reality and indicative of a sociopath's attempt to provide justification.

Just exactly how gruesome were the murders? Gruesome beyond comprehension, just ghastly. How could a robbery turn into a bizarre event that captivated the attention of an entire nation? What was the real motive behind the events? Why was each family member bound in an inhuman manner? Why was each family member gagged? Why was each family member in a different part of the house? Did my brother and Perry have a need to separate the family members to make sure they could be in control of the situation? Did the family members struggle at all? Did they plead for mercy?

Investigators say there was no evidence that the Clutter family put up a struggle. If so, why not? These details may not seem important, but they are to me because I want to understand my brother. Many other questions remain unanswered. What I hope to do in this book is to answer some of the questions I raised through the choices I made and through my pitiful behavior following the murders that hurt my own family so much. I hope that by telling my story I can provide answers to my family and take a step toward redemption.

Chapter Two
Looking Back To Childhood

When one thinks of Kansas, a typical reaction is to think of Dorothy in the movie *Wizard of Oz*. While that is a delightful way to view the locale in which I lived as a child, I had nothing magical to return me to my peaceful and normal life after the tragic Clutter murders. The life I knew as serene and quite ordinary ceased to exist after the strange turn of events in 1959. The events left my parents and me utterly shattered in mind, soul, and spirit for the rest of our days. "Normal," "peaceful" and "sane" would be words that would elude all of us for a lifetime.

How does a person's life change so dramatically? I cannot believe even to this day how fast my life changed that winter. We went from being normal folks to people who were considered dangerous, vile, and perhaps evil. I still remember the sick feeling I would get in my stomach when I realized that I was connected to one of the most evil and horrific crimes of the century. I was no angel by any means, but I would never have harmed anyone in the world. It was not in my nature to do so.

After all the publicity surrounding the crime and I was judged guilty by association with my brother, my mind continued to reel from the heartache and pain. I lacked control of the events following the murders. Confused, I could not fully comprehend what was happening. I was constantly at a loss for words, hiding from people and their dreadful reactions to the Hickock name.

Ours was a simple story that began with the typical small town American experience in the 1950s. I had both a mother and father in my home. How they loved one another was evident in the way in which they lived. They were not fancy folk. They were not poor folk. They were not rich folk. They were ordinary in every sense of the word. The relationship they shared was one that focused on family, their sons, and the beautiful pastoral setting of farm life in Kansas. They taught my brother and me the joy of living off the land, the beauty of nature, and the rewards of working and playing hard.

My dad, Walter Samuel Hickock, was a reflection of his own honest red-haired German-speaking mother, who believed in the importance and the strength of family. He was not a particularly religious individual, but he was a dedicated, hard-working mechanic and auto body repair technician who made a decent living for his family. He took great pride in being noted as one of the best auto body repair persons in the business. My mom, Eunice, was an attractive woman. She dedicated her time to being a homemaker and to her efforts in her Christian beliefs. If she could have driven a car, she would have attended her Methodist church every day. She had a great longing for spiritual peace, and she reflected this peace in our lives.

During my parents' early years together, my dad had tried a number of jobs in order to provide for his family. We lived in Kansas City before moving in 1946 to Edgerton, Kansas, a town located forty miles away. The move to Edgerton was a direct result of the realization on my dad's part that he wanted more peace in his life. He thought that perhaps in Edgerton he could find the peace that he had experienced in childhood. I have heard that people often return to their roots. Perhaps this is what my dad was trying to do when he began searching for the perfect country property for his family. He enlisted the assistance of Miles Stephens, a lawyer in Kansas City, who was a man of color with integrity and high respectability, to complete the necessary transactions and paperwork. Dad very seldom needed the assistance of a lawyer. Little did he realize that

Miles Stephens would be a source of reference in a future time of great distress.

The property in Edgerton was picturesque and thickly wooded. I will never forget the first time Dad brought us to see our new family place. It seemed like a forest to us. There was no road and a lush stand of trees blocked any kind of passage into the property. On that first trip, I remember the summer beauty of the property. It was as though the sun was shining on our happiness. Both Mom and Dad were pleased to secure their own farmland and embark on a new way of living.

Mom and Dad had birthed four sons: Richard Eugene Hickock, a set of twins that died at birth, and me, Walter David Hickock. Dad believed the land would provide a place of residence as well as income and recreation for the family. The land consisted of forty-four acres without any structures, not even a family dwelling. Before building a home, Dad enlisted our help to clear trees in order to complete a road into the property. We were taught every cost-saving technique in our work at fashioning a homestead. For instance, we recovered stones from the stream that was on the property and hand-carried them to the entrance of the property. After securing a large number of stones, the county workers were asked to crush our stones, so we could have gravel for the road that would lead to our home. They willingly complied and thus we had a graveled passageway to the area in which we were to build.

The memory of our first residence makes me smile as I fondly remember Dad's efforts at "putting a roof over our heads." Upon moving the family to the new homestead, a tent was set up to establish living quarters for the family while the farm home was being built. While that may seem like a strange thing to do today, my dad was an independent man. He wanted to build his own house and live off the land. He definitely accomplished that goal. Living in the tent prior to the actual building of the house was somewhat of an adventure. Curtains formed partitions between our beds. Canvas was put on our bedding to keep it dry. We lived in the tent for about three months or so. It must have been very difficult on my mom since she was a city girl, but I never once heard her complain.

As well as pastures for cows, the farmland was utilized for fields of corn, milo, wheat, hay, and strawberry patches. Dad continued in his job and worked our land with our help after working hours. We always had a garden full of the best vegetables, such as potatoes, sweet corn, bell peppers, green beans, a variety of berries, onions, and the like. My mom would preserve our vegetables by the difficult process of canning, so we always had vegetables from the garden in the winter months. The few horses we owned were used for work since the family did not own a tractor. The same horses provided recreation for my brother and me as we rode them freely in our spare time. The stream that ran through the property provided opportunities for fishing and swimming.

Our house, once it was completed, had no running water and was heated by a butane stove. At first we carried water from the stream, heated it outside, and then brought it in for baths. Later, a well was dug. The well was so welcome, especially in providing water for the gardens and the horses. None of this seemed unusual to us. It did not seem hard; it was just the way we lived. We always considered ourselves very fortunate to have property, a home, and a place that allowed us to work hard, play, and live well.

My brother and I attended Kansas City Elementary School and went on to graduate from high school. We did what many families did at that time, spending our energies at working, living right, and enjoying the peaceful setting of the Kansas countryside. We did what many brothers do, occasionally getting into arguments of one type or another. There was a six-year age difference between Dick and me, so in my younger years, my dad would correct Dick and usually whip him if he took advantage of me.

As we got older, Dad was never afraid to discipline us. I remember my last whipping at age sixteen or eighteen. Mom never had to discipline much since Dad was so strong. I never remember Mom having any type of disagreement with Dick. When Dad and Dick argued, it was usually about the places that Dick wanted the freedom to frequent. Usually, if Dick wanted something, he managed to find a way to get it. He was very strong-willed.

During high school days, other boys from the local school would come over and eagerly help with all the chores. After the chores, they would be allowed to enjoy hunting, fishing, swimming, or walking through the woods with us. I used to smile when I realized that they were so willing to work just to enjoy what my brother and I enjoyed every day of our lives.

Many family and friends often gathered to cook and visit at our family homestead. The meals were always cooked on the wood stove outside and then served outside, no matter how large or small the crowd or the season. There was very little consumption of alcoholic beverages. Baseball games were usually organized for any child or adult interested in playing. At the end of the day's activities, guests would remain in the tent that had previously housed our family. The family gatherings continued all year long, in sunshine, rain, or snow. I look back on these wonderful gatherings of people at our home and cherish the memories of safe and happy days. At no time during this period could I have anticipated the shadows that would envelop our lives.

Wintertime activities included pheasant hunting trips in west Kansas with my dad and Dick. These hunting trips were common at that time for all men of the area and revolved around shared companionship, the sport of spotting the wild game, and bringing food home to the family. Incidentally, the last pheasant hunting adventure took place exactly one week before November 15, 1959. I remember when we first heard about the murders and Dick's possible connection; I mistakenly thought that he could not have been involved because I thought the murders occurred on the weekend of our last hunting trip. Dick was hunting that fateful night of November 15, but not for pheasants.

This life was a life so similar to many families living in America in the 1950s and early '60s. Where is the ending that states "and they lived happily ever after"? Our story takes a horrific turn. None of us as family members could have possibly seen signs of what was to come. The people of Edgerton could never have predicted that the community would produce a murderer. I never could have understood the anger that Edgerton would direct at my family and me.

Likewise, a town named Holcomb never had any warning of the notoriety that was to come its way. No one could have comprehended the magnitude of the chain of events that were to follow the crimes of one terrible night. Could anyone have possibly understood that one event would change the lives of virtually everyone that had any connection with the massacre? Never in my wildest dreams could I have understood how dreadfully our lives would change and how our world would become shattered and distorted. My family would never return to the idyllic life we had previously loved and enjoyed.

Chapter Three
A Murderer In Our Midst

Richard was a normal young boy who grew to be an outstanding athlete with a pleasant personality. Even after high school, we both continued to live with our parents on our farm until we got married. We continued to hunt and fish together, and worked at our respective jobs. When did such a radical change come upon Dick?

After a lifetime of reflection upon our lives before the murders, I realize that there were signs that could have foretold of possible potential problems. Yet, how was I to know that the changes occurring in Dick could negatively affect so many lives? I first noticed changes in my brother's actions when Dick was in the latter part of high school. Dick was normally a fun-loving person who was never in any trouble.

However, there was a first episode that revealed the troubled spirit of my brother. Dick stole a watch from a local drugstore. I remember when it happened that my parents were shocked Dick would do such a thing. Dick readily admitted his guilt. He made restitution and no charges were filed. After speaking with Dick about the theft, I believe my parents, who were honest and law-abiding people, thought he was just trying to do something different, merely seeking peer approval. Had they known that this was just the beginning of a downward spiraling of decadent behavior, they would have been frightened beyond belief.

Another incident in Dick's life that could possibly be a key to the radical changes in behavior involved a car wreck. This incident occurred while Dick was dating Carol, whom he eventually married. Water on the highway caused him to lose control of his car. He was ejected from the car, landed in a water-filled ditch, and nearly drowned. The passenger with Dick flagged down another vehicle. An ambulance arrived to take them both to the hospital in Gardner, Kansas.

The damage caused to Dick's face as a result of the accident left his face looking "off-balance." His left eye seemed to have sunk in his head. The doctor did not say the accident had impaired Dick's vision in any way, but Dick had to wear a white patch over his eye for quite some time. Dick once told me that he could not see as clearly as he did before the accident. The doctor was just satisfied in having saved the eye, because he thought for a time that Dick might lose sight in that eye. Dick did not look grotesque; he just looked like his face no longer had balance.

A more serious consequence of the wreck was its affect on Dick's attitude. He was deeply upset that his "good looks" had been altered. Always the attractive ladies man, Dick found it quite unacceptable to have a distorted appearance. Yet, he continued in his quest for women, and women were still attracted to him, despite the change in his appearance. His smile seemed to be the winning card with women. In fact, when Dick smiled, his face seemed to even out and the eye injury was not as noticeable.

At the age of nineteen, Dick married Carol, an attractive and vivacious blonde girl of sixteen, whom he adored. Dick worked at Santa Fe Railways at the time of the marriage, but later drove an ambulance because it provided a better income. They had three children and Dick seemed settled in his marriage.

But what seemed to be true was far from the truth. It was not until recently that I came to understand what Carol had been through during the hard times of marriage to my brother. In 2005, I began searching for answers to what happened in 1959. One of my first attempts was when I went to see Carol, Dick's first wife, at her home in August 2005. She more than willingly gave insight into my brother, and the insight was quite revealing. I knew Carol to be an honest Christian person, so I knew she would share sincerely with me. Carol reminded me that when she married Dick, he was a good person. He had only one speeding ticket and supported the family effectively.

She calmly explained: *"One of the reasons I found Dick attractive was that he had personality plus. Everyone who knew Dick really liked him. He had a way of just talking and being comfortable with anyone. He was an individual who found humor in everything and he shared this humor with all around him. My early years with Dick were good, but not necessarily easy. Dick was always a very good provider. He made me believe in myself. He always told me what a beautiful and wonderful person I was. He had a way of making me feel like an extraordinary woman. This was the problem, however. He used that same tactic with other women. He absolutely was always a womanizer. The reason for the divorce was that although he loved me he loved any other woman he could."*

I had known that Dick was a flirt in high school, but I thought he had the perfect marriage. Carol gave me an insight into my brother's actions that I evidently had not ever accepted or fully understood.

Carol continued describing Dick: *"Dick was an excellent father. No matter how late he returned home at night, he would hold our boys and rock them. He showed great affection for our children. I loved watching him play with our boys. His closeness to our children was one of the reasons I tried to keep my marriage intact. Dick was never abusive in a physical manner with me. Yet, I came to realize another type of abuse, the mental abuse of a constant fear of another woman's presence in our relationship. The other women in Dick's life were very apparent. The other women were the reason that I decided to divorce Dick.*

I was fearful that if I tolerated Dick's behavior, my children would eventually lose respect for me. Worse than that fact, I was fearful that the boys would learn the same negative patterns of behavior from their father and repeat his mistakes when they became adults. I readily admit that Dick loved me as much as he was capable of loving. He just loved other women at the same time he was my husband."

15

Carol's deep regrets were evident when she sadly shared that her children were all under the age of seven at the time of the murders. All these many years later, I am moved by the vivid description of Dick as a loving father. But since Dick and I spent a great deal of time together, I, more than anyone else, could see a change in his thinking even at that time. The change hinged on his already erratic behavior. After the stay in the hospital because of the accident, Dick became totally different from the easygoing and carefree individual I had known all my life. His demeanor was more solemn, morose, and extremely reckless. He believed that he was able to do and say anything without any consequences.

Dick continued conducting his life in an unmanageable manner. He stopped all his pursuits in the areas of recreational sports. His attitude continued to become more defiant and increasingly restless. His sporadic and irrational words left the rest of us wondering if the concussion he suffered in the accident had resulted in trauma to his brain. There were so many things he said and did that went totally against our old-fashioned and disciplined upbringing. He seemed, at times, to be in his own angry state of mind, sometimes outspoken and other times silent.

It was during this time that Dick became so involved with another woman that he and Carol divorced. He married the new woman in his life. While married to her, Dick had another encounter with law enforcement. Dick stole a gun and was arrested. He was sentenced to the Lansing Penitentiary for approximately seventeen months. While in prison, Dick's second wife filed for divorce.

I was beginning to wonder who Dick was and why he was determined to do the unacceptable things he did. We were told when Dick's father-in-law, who was a minister, went to talk with officials at the penitentiary about his concerns regarding Dick's mental state, officials extended Dick's stay at the Kansas State Penitentiary in Lansing. I suppose Dick's father-in-law was more perceptive than most people, for he knew that Dick was not rehabilitating in the manner that he should.

Eventually, Dick was released and his personality difficulties were more pronounced. I still wonder if the authorities had detained

Dick and provided him with the psychiatric assistance he needed, whether his behavior might have improved. In the years since my brother's accident and the radical change in his personality, modern science has learned much about organic causes of brain dysfunction and the complications caused due to scarring lesions. Could my brother have been an example of some undiagnosed problem that stemmed from trauma to the brain as a result of the accident? This leaves much to question in all our minds.

Dick began working at a body shop in Olathe, Kansas. It was during this period after his release from the penitentiary that Dick often told me of things he wanted to do. They were bad things, evil things. They remained shocking to me each time he spoke of them. His demeanor and spirit was that of someone very foreign to me. He had the words "death" or "hate" branded on his fingers, though I cannot remember which. He also had other tattoos that were not there before his prison stay.

While in prison he began lifting weights. I thought this was a good way to exercise and build muscles. Upon his release from prison, I lifted weights with him. He was still my hero, although he was altered in so many ways. I had always admired and respected him. He was a good friend. The memories of playing ball, riding horses, or swimming in our stream both strengthen and sadden me these many years later. I kept trying to be close to him to maintain the relationship we had before the accident and before the prison time, but it became increasingly difficult. I would have done anything to bring my brother back to our peaceful reality, but, in my opinion, I thought he no longer understood reality.

Chaper Four
The Gun And The Guilt

My eagerness to help bring my brother back to reality played a large part in the crime that was to occur on November 15, 1959. I still cringe when I think of the role I played in the murders. It began innocently enough and I was so happy to be able to do a favor for my brother that I did not consider the repercussions of my actions. My refusal to accommodate Dick when he asked me if I would do him a big favor could have changed the course of events that followed. While this sounds melodramatic, I have spent years wondering if life would be different had I told my brother simply, "No, I'd better not go and do something like that for you … at least not until I know you are okay." Instead, when Dick asked if I would purchase a gun for him, I made all the arrangements, including the money for the gun. I remember asking if he needed a particular brand of gun, but he told me that it simply did not matter.

The real story about the gun is different from news articles or books about the murders. Some said it was my father's gun. Some said my parents had purchased it. The truth lies simply in the fact that since Dick was an ex-convict, he was not allowed to purchase a weapon. He came to me and asked if I would buy him a gun. It was prior to pheasant hunting season because he alluded to the fact that we could begin hunting together again. I gladly accepted the task of purchasing a gun. Never in my wildest dreams could I have ever imagined the pain I would undergo in my lifetime for that afternoon of shopping.

In my mind, I thought Dick was finally getting better and ready to share hunting adventures again. I even thought this might help Dad out since he had not been feeling well. A hunting trip might perk Dad up! Our past hunting trips had been so much of an adventure. All three of us would plan hunting expeditions in which we would travel to western Kansas, where pheasants were plentiful. The trips were always good because we shared them, cooked over campfires, and competed to see who could shoot the most game. I wanted to believe that Dick was finally getting back to his old self. For this I was grateful! I purchased the gun.

I was in my early twenties. I was making good money working at Taylor Forge Pipe Works, so I decided I would buy the gun as a gift for my brother. I figured I could probably put the gun on layaway, if need be. I can clearly remember walking into the Coast to Coast Store in Paola, Kansas. The gun was priced in the range of seventy-five to one hundred dollars. I do not remember if I paid for it in one lump sum or if I put in on layaway. It was a Savage 12-gauge, pump-action shotgun, Model 10. I bought it brand-new and remember that the barrel had a blue coating. I even remember my pride in thinking I was doing something that might help my brother.

I also very distinctly remember the events of the afternoon after work when I picked up the gun, put it in my car, and delivered it to my mom and dad's house. The afternoon was not remarkable in any way. The sun was shining as I drove to my parents' home. I kept thinking that Dick would be really glad that I had bought the gun for him. I also began thinking, as most hunters do, of the enjoyment we would have on our next pheasant-hunting trip. The main reason I brought the gun to Mom and Dad's was because I knew that Dick was living there.

It is so strange when I think about my part in buying the gun and the fact that no one ever questioned me about it. I do not even know if law enforcement officials ever checked out the fact that I had bought the gun used in the murders. I suppose times were different back then, but my role as an unwitting accomplice was never considered. That is, not to my knowledge! I know that things would be different today. A more thorough investigation would have been done and I would have been interrogated. I do not understand why they did not investigate certain aspects of the crime. I certainly would later read about other details of the crime being thoroughly considered in news articles about it and in Truman Capote's book *In Cold Blood.*

I remember the exact moment Dick took the gun from Mom and Dad's house and went outside to use it for the first time. It was in the evening. Dick was very pleased with the new gun and he began pumping it in the front yard. It was then that Dick made an unusual remark that did not mean a thing to me at the time, but is embedded in my mind today. Dick said, "There will be no witnesses!"

This was a very strange remark, and I had no idea what Dick meant by it. It made me uneasy, though, and it still haunts me to this day. I look back and think how foolish I was to blindly believe everything my brother told me. Did I not know that he had changed from the person I knew to this totally irrational man who had served time in prison? Yes, I knew all the facts, but I suppose I was in some type of denial or just not smart enough to figure there was a problem.

I think that if I had just known that his remark was a sign that something was terribly wrong, then perhaps I could have changed the future course of events. I still keep asking myself the question, *"How did I not know?"* I just wish I would have asked Dick the questions, *"What are you talking about? What witnesses?"* Maybe I could have obtained help for him. Something was really wrong about his words and his actions, and I did absolutely nothing to change what was to happen!

Not long after the remarks about "no witnesses," Dick made another questionable comment. He stated to me, *"Maybe we will not have to worry about money much longer."* I just could not imagine what Dick was talking about. I did know that our family was struggling financially with medical bills due to Dick's hospital stay and with my dad constantly being ill. I did not understand these statements and I did not ask him to explain them to me. How often I wished I had asked what he meant!

When the authorities questioned my parents after the murders, my parents said they had no recollection of anything unusual regarding the gun. Dick had nonchalantly removed the gun from their home at some time prior to the Clutter murders. This would not have raised a suspicion of any kind from my parents. Seeing either of us take a gun could only mean that we were going out to the woods to hunt rabbit or to practice shooting. No questions would have been asked. I do not think my parents could remember exactly when Dick removed the gun from the house and put it in the car.

I wish that I had put two-and-two together, but I had no idea that Dick had any intention of frightening or harming anyone. I still rationalize my purchase of that gun because, at the time, I firmly believed that my brother, my dad, and I would once again enjoy the late fall pheasant hunting season.

Perhaps I should have given the request more thought. After all, my brother had gone to jail and upon his release he was acting rather peculiar. Still, I knew in my heart he loved hunting. I never knew Dick to be the kind of person to deliberately hurt anyone. If I had considered for one moment that his use of the gun would be for any illegal, immoral, or unjust purpose, I certainly would not have entertained the idea of buying it.

After I found out my brother was directly involved in the murders, I was shocked, embarrassed, and completely in disbelief. When I finally asked Dick if all the stories on television were true, he shrugged and simply said, *"Not all of them."* According to Dick, the story of that fateful night had many of the same components that we heard on television, but he knew other details that only appeared in his version of the story. Yet, my rationalizations for buying the gun cannot undo the irreparable damage that took place at the hands of Perry Smith and my brother.

Chapter Five
News Of Tragedy

On Sunday evening, November 15, 1959, my dad, Dick, and I were watching a basketball game on television when news of an entire family being murdered in Holcomb, Kansas, was announced. The news report stated that no one had been arrested and that investigations were ongoing. Since Holcomb was across the state from Edgerton, the only reaction from my dad was to say, *"That was a terrible thing to happen."* I agreed with my father. Dick sat silently, never commenting one way or other, and continued to watch the basketball game for a short while. He then left the room. Neither my dad nor I noticed anything unusual about his demeanor. He displayed no overt reaction to the news.

As we soon learned, the murders had been horribly gruesome. The crime quickly grabbed national attention. It was a frightening event because, unlike the news of today, gruesome and horrific crimes were not as common. I think back and speculate that Dick must have been astounded that he was associated with a tragedy that had made national news. As I remember those days, I really wonder if Dick's state of mind was so demented that he did not understand the gravity of the matter. Was he so far removed from reality that he disassociated himself?

Dick was soon busy at work or traveling about on one of his adventures. We never quite knew what his adventures entailed. In fact, he left home on November 21, 1959, on one of these adventures just six days after the murders. We had become accustomed to Dick's strange behavior ever since his release from the Kansas State Penitentiary, now known as Lansing Correctional Facility.

In December, after the news broke concerning the murders of the Clutter family in Holcomb, police officers came to my parents' home to inquire about Dick's whereabouts. I was married and had moved to my own home, and I was surprised when police officers also came to my house in search of Dick. I believed the inquiry had to do with something simple, like writing bad checks. Dick was often writing bad checks wherever he went. At that point, I had no idea that my brother could possibly be wanted for a violent crime. I remember wondering why the police exhibited gruff and serious attitudes. Never in my wildest imaginings did I think that Dick could possibly be involved in anything as serious as the taking of the life of another human being. Nor could I have comprehended that he would have been involved in the taking of four lives, two of whom were children!

It was the sheriff from Olathe, Kansas, who seemed to have a distinct dislike for Dick and made it his personal business to prowl around outside my parents' home in the evenings. I guess he was trying to find clues to Dick's whereabouts. At least at the time, we judged him to be sneaking about, but perhaps, he was just being a good investigative officer seeking clues to unravel one of America's most sensational and violent crimes.

One such incident with the sheriff that I clearly remember occurred when my dad went to the backdoor with a shotgun in hand one evening. He approached the sheriff to ask what his business was. A rather stunned sheriff merely stated that he believed Dick was in the vicinity and he wanted to talk with him. My dad had trouble understanding what the sheriff could possibly want with his son and why he would choose to prowl about in the evening in his search. Dad called me and together we pondered what the root of the sheriff's suspicions might be.

My family had not yet connected Dick with the unthinkable murders in Holcomb, Kansas. Dick was notorious for writing bad checks. Naturally, we were under the impression that the authorities were interested in stopping Dick for that or for some other parole violation. The police officers finally told Dad and Mom that Dick was wanted for a much more serious offense. My parents called me immediately to share their concern. They were still not told that Dick was a suspect, but in just a few short weeks we all would be told the specifics. That revelation was the defining moment when our lives changed drastically, and that drastic change lasted forever.

We began to reflect on Dick's prison stay. When Dick was released, he did seem more like a hardened criminal, and he had made connections with other criminals. It was in prison that he met a fellow inmate named Perry Smith, a man originally from Harrington, Elko County, Nevada. Perry was raised with parents who fought often and finally divorced. We came to find out quite a lot about him as the news reports covered intimate details of the lives of Perry Smith and my brother. Perry was involved in gangs while in his teens and spent time in detention centers. He was in constant trouble even when serving time in the service. Perry later was convicted of grand larceny, escaping from jail, and burglary, and was sentenced to five to ten years. A friendship that began in prison was plainly doomed from the beginning.

After their release from prison, Perry Smith and Dick Hickock should never have made contact because doing so would have immediately violated their paroles. My brother was the one who invited him to Kansas. He even asked my mom if he could stay at their house. Mom had a bad feeling about Perry and refused to let him stay. That refusal never stopped the relationship that was ongoing with the two men. They had adventures planned and places to travel. They did whatever they wanted. The chemistry of their combined personalities proved to be lethal.

Chapter Six
Finally An Arrest

Police officers continued to ask my parents and me probing questions about Dick and his whereabouts. We honestly had no information to give them, but they did not believe us. They continued clandestine surveillance of our homes. I knew they were trying to apprehend my brother. Perhaps they thought we were hiding him. I do not know, but being watched was a frightening experience.

Perry Smith went his own way after the night of the murders, and Dick came back home to Edgerton. When news of the crime broke, both men reunited and began running together starting on November 21. They went from state to state living life on the wild side and writing bad checks to fund their spree. They traveled to a variety of places, such as Las Vegas, Mexico, and Florida.

My parents and I wanted to continue to believe that Dick had broken parole by writing bad checks. We did not fully grasp the reason for continual visits from police officers. We continued to believe that they thought we were hiding Dick. None of us knew where he had gone or exactly why! At some point in December, my dad just asked why Dick was being investigated, and the police told us that he might have a connection to the Clutter murders.

Bad checks were embarrassing enough, but being connected to a crime of this proportion could never have entered our minds. As I mentioned earlier, when I was first told of this news I remember a brief moment of relief. In calculating the weekend that the murders occurred, I honestly thought that Dad, Dick, and I had been on a pheasant-hunting trip. Sorry to say, I was mistaken about the dates of the hunting trip … that trip had taken place the weekend before the murders. My relief was short lived!

Later in December, I was actually relieved when Dick and Perry were arrested in Las Vegas, Nevada. They had been evading the police and were enjoying what they called the good life. I was relieved because I still believed that perhaps my brother had been misjudged. At that time, I really thought there had to be some kind of mistake. I wanted to believe in his innocence.

Yet, how could I continue to try avoiding any association with the awful Clutter murders? I certainly did not want my only brother to be responsible for them. I remember Christmas that year as being a sad and desolate time for my family. No joy and no excitement existed in our hearts or in our lives. Fear and shame permeated our day-to-day existence. My first wife and I did manage to share presents with my children in our humble home in Paola, Kansas. I watched as they sat among their few presents with the lights flickering on our Christmas tree. It was at this time that I decided I had to tell them the truth about Dick.

I began by saying that Uncle Dick had done something terribly wrong. I also told them that they would probably not be seeing him for Christmas. Not seeing him would have been a hurtful thing. My children were as everyone else when it came to Dick. They loved the magic he brought when he came to share time with us. He knew how to be a child. As young as they were, my children adored him.

As I struggled to find the words to tell my children the truth, I wondered how hard it would become for them to be Hickocks in the state of Kansas. The crime and all its elements were quickly growing into the biggest news event of the day. There was no way to hide or shelter my children from the truth they would have to face on the playground at school, at ball games, or even when attending church. Somehow, I believed that if I told them all of the truth, it would hurt them as much as others talking about the ugliness of the murders. I remember their young and innocent faces. I remember that I was so ashamed for our family and so afraid of the pain they would feel from knowing the truth about their uncle.

There was no big Christmas gathering at my parents' home. I think I had already begun the process of distancing myself from my parents. It had become the only way I could manage the pain I felt for them. My pitiful parents, conscientious law-abiding citizens, were shocked that their son was a wanted man. Both of my parents cried continuously. This bizarre change of events in our lives changed them forever. They became melancholy and depressed individuals. I worried about them each and every day. They were ashamed, embarrassed, and frightened.

The harassing phone calls were endless. There were calls from people screaming that we were evil. We were condemned because Dick was of our blood. No one trusted us. I believed my friends and acquaintances wanted nothing to do with me. With some, that attitude was evident. With others, I may have just been paranoid. I know that people were afraid to trust us with even simple, ordinary conversations. We, too, had a hard time trusting ourselves. How could we have not known that a murderer lived among us?

My thoughts ran rampant trying to discern the situation. How could my brother have orchestrated the entire chain of events? I tried to figure out how it all began. I quickly learned from the investigators' reports that Dick's first knowledge of the Clutter safe came from a fellow inmate, a man named Floyd Wells. Wells was still in prison when he heard of the murders, and he told his story to the warden. Wells said that while he and Dick were cell mates, he had shared with Dick a layout of the Clutter home and a map to the Clutter homestead in Holcomb. Wells seemed to believe that the Clutters were so wealthy that their safe had to be full of cash.

Had Dick intentionally planned to do harm or did he really intend to just rob the place? If robbery was the motive, why did Dick get Perry Smith involved and why did he bring a gun? These and many other questions remained unanswered. What had happened to Dick to make him think and act like a criminal? Would people ever leave us alone? What was to happen to us? Would people blame us for Dick's involvement in the murders? Would Dick get a fair trial?

Would Dick be safe in prison? Would Dick end up hanging for his crimes? Would my family ever feel like "normal" people again?

The questions were endless. We had no answers. Even if we had had answers, I do not think that we could have comprehended the demise of our normalcy. The answers that were to come in the upcoming years would bring pain beyond belief into all of our lives. Never could any of us even verbalize the fact that we had a murderer in our family.

In May 2007, an investigative reporter from Sarasota, Florida, contacted me regarding similar murders that occurred shortly after the Clutters were killed. The reporter sent me articles about a murder case involving the Walker family, and I noted that there were some similarities. The reporter was wondering if Dick and Perry could possibly be connected to the case since it was known that they had traveled through Florida during December 1959. It seemed that some DNA samples from the murders were available, and the reporter and the police wanted to see if my DNA might prove to be a match. If was, they could possibly close this cold case because it would establish the fact that my brother was at the crime scene.

Later, someone from a Florida crime lab called me to set the DNA test up, but I told him, *"Sure, you can have my DNA sample, but I want you to know you'd better bring two checkbooks."* I am ashamed of what I told him. Was I serious or was I joking? I don't even know now. I realized afterward that saying this was very wrong. I was not contacted again.

Could Dick possibly have been associated with other crimes? The thought still sends chills down my spine. What if the police or a reporter could connect my brother to those murders? Does it matter all these years later; my brother has been dead for over forty years. I even felt sorry for the Walker family. Could I have possibly helped them bring closure to their grief?

I now wish I had taken a more serious approach to the matter. I could have talked with our local sheriff to see if I should go ahead with providing a DNA sample. I am so remorseful that I did not actively pursue being of assistance to the investigative reporter to see if there was a possibility my brother also had a connection to the Walker case.

It has taken me many years to finally say that as I sift through articles and my own thoughts about the crime, I readily admit that my brother could not possibly be as innocent as he portrayed himself to be. He must have meditated on the plan a number of times. He must have thought about every single detail. When the murders occurred, I wanted to believe the best of my brother, the brother that I so admired. The facts remained … hard and real: My brother was indeed a murderer.

Chapter Seven
Immediate And Unrelenting Notoriety

I realized from the first news of my brother's association with the Clutter murders that he was involved in a deed that was unimaginable. The realization that four people, including a father, a mother, and their two children had been murdered in such a brutal manner was heart wrenching. At the time, the sordid Clutter murders ranked among the most horrendous of such crimes to have occurred in the United States. Today, we are jaded by multiple, gory murders constantly before our eyes. I guess the fear can be compared to the feelings of our nation when faced with 9/11. The word terrorist was not a word used often in 1959, but the murders brought terror to people in a way not known before. My brother and his friend were the terrorists!

The terrorist attack in New York is used here to explain a point. Of course, many more people died that sad day in September 2001. That awful day still haunts America. The comparison is that the entire nation stood shocked, angry, and completely out of control with feelings of helplessness. When I think back about the many small towns in the United States and the comfortable lives people lived in the 1950s, I can only shudder to think how the Clutter murders rattled many people and changed their sense of security.

Both events involved innocent people that did not deserve to die such horrible deaths, and both events stemmed from people who were angry and misguided in their thinking. I think about the victims in the September 11 attacks, the many victims, who did not die but were left to move forward with their lives. My compassion for the victims and families of 9/11 resulted from my own feelings of being left with only my parents to endure the consequences of my brother's actions. I lost family members. No, they did not die immediately. They all died a slow, painful death each day living through the enormity of shame and devastating embarrassment. The agony of watching my parents often masked my own pain and anger. These forty plus years later I can assure you my relentless anguish still haunts me. Later, when Truman Capote wrote the book about the murders, I must say that he was a genius in bringing forth a title that rang with such clarity … *In Cold Blood.*

Immediate notoriety for my family was more than just a difficult situation. Edgerton was a small, close-knit community. The citizens had no doubt of Richard Hickock's guilt, for they knew of his past deeds and his dealings with law enforcement officials. The anger of the local people was indescribable. The phone calls continued day and night to both my parents' home and to mine, with many callers repeating questions, such as, *"Has any of your family died yet?" "You and all your family should die like the Clutters?"* or *"Why don't you go out west and get killed?"* The phone rang continually with calls from irate people. Perhaps some of these calls came from outside our community. I will never know for sure.

A phone call from one minister went something like this: *"I am a minister. I think it is my duty to tell you that you and your family should all die!"* Other calls involved people screaming at us over the phone yelling obscenities or threatening our lives. Perhaps we *should* have died because I can tell you our lives were never to be the same. We died a little every day as we tried to survive the aftermath of the murders. I still hear those voices almost fifty years later. I still remember the hurtful expressions and the fear on my parents' faces. They asked themselves repeatedly if they could have done something differently in raising Dick. My mom prayed continuously and never gave up in her efforts to understand the gravity of the situation. She never gave up in praying for a miracle.

There was no way to ever get away from the crime. Television stations continued detailed coverage of the murders almost constantly. This was the most sensational crime of the period, as I have said. Since everyone knew me in the small community in which I lived and worked, people felt comfortable asking me questions. The questions were both sincere and inquisitive. The questions also hurt to the very core of my being. They wanted to know how my parents were faring through the ordeal, how Dick was doing in jail, the outcome of any legal assistance, what Dick's motives were, and other similar questions. The questions never stopped. It mattered not if I was at work, shopping, or just running errands about town. People wanted to know what was going on and they asked me every question imaginable. I started trying to avoid contact with anyone.

I was working at Taylor Forge and Pipe Works in Paola near my family home. That close-knit community was much like Edgerton. Its citizens were really compassionate with Dick when he first had a run-in with the law after stealing a watch. Then when Dick was in trouble a second time for stealing a gun, the consensus of the community was that the law enforcement officials were much too hard on him. They were astounded that he received a sentence of jail time. They were supportive of my parents and me with comments of their concern for Dick and my family.

However, when news of the murders broke, the communities in which we had lived and worked were enraged with Dick Hickock. Who could possibly blame them for reacting in this manner? The stigma and angry remarks changed me forever. I began to wrestle with a feeling of paranoia. I did not even know what that word meant at the time. It has only been in recent years that I understand that I was extremely paranoid. Some asked prying questions, some were just downright rude, and others ignored me as if I were the murderer.

I became so ashamed I looked away as others passed me on the street or in the grocery store. My stomach tightened when people inquired about any member of my family. A simple question like *"How is your mother doing?"* would throw me into a cold sweat. What was I supposed to say? I could not say, *"Just dandy!"*

I looked around before I would enter a business or a hamburger place to make sure that I could avoid the glances and stares of people who made me feel like an outsider. It was so confusing because these were the people that made my town such a friendly and peaceful community. Now, they were my enemies. I just wanted to be left alone. Then again, I wanted someone to rescue me. Even at work, I just wanted to do my job and not speak. I was lonely and cold inside of my being every day after those murders.

I felt so badly about the entire situation, but I was never one for being able to express myself. I sometimes tried to answer the many questions, but there were no right answers. The fact that Dick was involved in anything so vile was unimaginable to me. Sometimes, I just walked away from the questioners, the menacing looks, and hushed tones in conversations. My personality deteriorated during these sad days. I never was so outgoing that I talked to everyone. I was just a regular guy who treated everyone with respect and believed that others would treat me with the same respect. My entire sense of who I was changed immediately. I became a person who was frightened of the very neighborhoods that I had known all my life. The loneliness has remained within me.

There were other times in which I knew that people had come to look at me differently. I felt an unusual amount of pressure from my association with a criminal who was also a member of my family. I found a set of tools on a road near my country home. Interstate 35 was being constructed at the time and I just figured the tools had to belong to one of the guys working on this new highway. I tried to find the owner by inquiring among the men who were in the area working on the new highway, but no one claimed the tools. I brought the tools to work hoping that someone would claim them.

After a while, I began using them. Not long after that, police came and arrested me for stealing the tools. Either one of two things had happened. I was being set up to have stolen goods in order to intimidate me into giving information about my brother that would assist law officials in determining by brother's motives. Another point of view is that perhaps law enforcement officials branded me a criminal based on my brother's misdeeds.

The pressure of being under constant scrutiny and ridicule led me to a desperate desire to run away from the reality of my life. I wanted to escape to a place where no one would know me. I wanted no more questions. I wanted to rid myself of the constant fear, shame, and embarrassment of being connected to the Clutter murders. It was at this time that I began a life of constant roaming in search of anonymity. Little did I know my initial attempt at running away would last almost my whole life.

Chapter Eight
Visit To See A Murderer

As I sat in the old 1938 Chevy in the early hours of a cold January morning in 1960 waiting for the car to warm up and for my dad to come from the house, I pondered about the travels planned for this day. In the past few months our lives went from routine and normal to extraordinary and unbelievable. We had arisen at 5:00 am and Mom had carefully prepared a breakfast of pancakes and bacon. Dad sat stoically in his chair, unspeaking, drinking his morning coffee.

It is strange that even now I can readily call to mind every element of our kitchen that morning. I can still smell the bacon and pancakes. I can still see the arrangement of the items in the center of the table. I can remember the floral housecoat my mom wore as she took considerable care to feed us before we ventured on our journey to visit my brother in jail. I can remember struggling to swallow my food. Looking at Dad, I knew he was making every attempt to eat his breakfast, the food his wife had prepared.

Who could eat with the heavy weight that lingered on our every thought and our every word? My poor mom was pathetic. She had become so depressed and downtrodden that she refused to come with us to visit Dick. I wondered if she was embarrassed, scared, or both. How does a mother come to terms with the fact that her child is a cold-blooded murderer?

When I left Mom and Dad in the kitchen, they were both acting as if they could not speak with me present. I slowly made my way to the car. My feet felt heavy as I walked that short distance. I quickly opened the door, tried to get comfortable, and began the wait for my dad. It seemed like time was standing still. Finally, I saw the kitchen door open and my dad leaned against the door frame. I wondered if the strength of the wood would give him strength. Dad had built our home as his own symbol of hope. Today, he needed hope. I needed hope. We were so scared.

I wondered if Dad was thinking about the reason he had purchased the farm. He had told us that he and Mom had chosen to simplify their lives. I wondered if he was contemplating how his dream had gone awry. My dad looked like he was in pain; Mom looked especially dejected and hopeless. She had been grieving since the day we found out my brother Dick was involved in one of the most heinous crimes of the century. Her despairing demeanor made me turn my head. I wanted to block out that image of my mother. All her inconsolable pain and her ever-increasing sorrow had robbed me of the mother I knew.

Had it only been weeks since our lives had been shattered with unbearable shame and misery? As I looked back at Mom, I realized that my dad was having a difficult time leaving her. I never knew if he lingered because he was so heartbroken for Mom or if fear was gripping his entire being for what we were to face this day. Today was a continuation of a nightmare that seemingly had no end.

The long seven-hour drive to Garden City, Kansas, would end in the final destination of the Garden City County Jail. Our goal was to see my brother who sat in a single jail cell. Had it only been days since Dick had been arrested for murder? It seemed more like months, maybe even years. The simplicity and enjoyment of living was gone. Within six weeks our lives were forever changed by one awful night! Our normal routines of living life and enjoying peace in our country home and its surrounding environment were never to return.

Dad made his way slowly toward the car. The look on his face was indisputable. It was a look of compassion for his bride and her pain, a pain that he could not erase. As he touched the handle on the car door, he stopped. Looking back toward the house, Dad lifted his hand gingerly in a slow, sad farewell. Upon entering the car and taking his place at the steering wheel, he quietly mentioned that it was nice weather that day. Putting the car in reverse, he remarked that we needed to stop for gas and oil and to check the tires for the journey from Edgerton to Garden City. Every word he uttered was laced with a sad, melancholy tone.

How quickly the disappointment had shown on Dad's face. His furrowed brow was a visible sign that he knew his life would never again be the same. My older brother was in very serious trouble. Looking back on it, there was little to prepare Dad for what he was now facing. He did not have the skills to deal with issues of this magnitude. He did not have the education or presence of mind to realize his need or my mom's need for psychological assistance during this time of crisis. The idea of seeing a psychologist was not acceptable because in those days mental illness was shameful. We had our own issues to face, but compounded with the community's reaction to Dick's crime, these issues made a terribly heavy burden for each of us to carry.

We each did what we could to survive, turning into ourselves since we didn't know how to help each other. Mom stopped attending church because she felt ostracized by people. Perhaps people thought their association with us would make them evil. Or perhaps people just did not know what to say to us.

I was a naïve young man in my twenties and was of little help to my parents. My own pain and embarrassment was more than I knew how to bear. I had no way of knowing how to cope with the overwhelming fear, anxiety, and guilt. The helplessness and the fear of the possible final outcome to this drama concerning Dick left us all feeling panic stricken. Dad and I tried to keep busy around the farm, but his health was failing. He continued to be different, so withdrawn. He seemed to have no energy. Our conversations and even the few meals I did share with them maintained a solemn air. I had my own reason for extreme guilt. After all, I had purchased the murder weapon. I do not believe my parents realized I had bought the gun and placed it in the house for Dick. They never talked with me or asked me about it.

We traveled for miles before my dad said another word. He finally mentioned that we would be taking the same roads that my brother and his accomplice had traveled on their way to the crime scene in Holcomb. My brother and Perry Smith had stopped in Emporia and visited a hardware store to buy supplies needed for the crime. They had also stopped at a drugstore intending to buy nylon stockings. These facts we knew because of the news reports.

As we drove to Garden City with the sun rising behind us in the eastern sky, I was frightened and elated to be able to see my brother. The fear was something that just stayed with me day and night. The elation was because I was going to see my brother, who was my friend. The many hours of driving gave us ample time to think. The route that we were navigating reminded us that we were traveling the route to the actual murder scene. Driving in silence leaves too much time for thinking … too much time. My own thoughts kept racing to the motivation for murder. How could my brother have possibly done this terrible deed? Why? Murder was an awful way to die. There was too much to understand and too much to try to decipher. Was there any way to make sense of all of this craziness?

Finally, my dad broke the silence and said, *"I just cannot understand why Dick would do anything like this. Do you have any idea why?"* This was a question that had been asked of me quite often in the recent days by people I worked with, old friends who knew us, and just about anybody brave enough to ask.

I simply said, *"Dad, it just had to be brought about by the company Dick kept while serving time in the penitentiary for stealing that gun."* That was all I could say. Dad then said: *"Dave, the few times Dick had been in trouble I just thought that they were, you know, a young man trying to get some attention. Your mom and I figured he would serve time and return to us ready to live a* decent *life."* Not much more was said because we had no more ideas about or reasons for Dick's actions.

My thoughts ran rampant as I sat in the car. Overwhelmed with guilt, I began wondering about the remarks that Dick had so aggressively expressed after his release from the penitentiary. *"There will be no witnesses." "Soon we will not have any money worries."* At the time he made these comments, I never took much stock in the words. I tried to make some sense out of those really strange remarks. I sat in silence because I knew that I shared the blame for what happened to the innocent Clutter family. I blamed myself for not telling anyone of Dick's remarks. Somehow, I was convinced that this crisis was at least partially my fault. I carry the guilt to this day, thinking that if I had been smarter I could have alerted someone about my brother's deranged thinking.

Perhaps, my dad had his own thoughts and regrets that he was standing guard over. He spoke with a controlled voice, but said very little as we traveled the many miles to Garden City. It was evident that he would slow down as he recognized a name of an establishment that the newspapers had named as a place where my brother and Perry had stopped on their journey to Holcomb. He must have tried to see or understand why they had stopped at the places they did. His brow remained furrowed for the entire trip. I looked over at him and realized that in just a few weeks my dad had become an old man.

Our visit to Garden City was to last for two to three days. It was a peaceful city, not remarkable to us in any way. Upon entering the town, I saw nothing unusual. There were few people on the streets. Those who were milling about were seemingly involved with their own affairs of life. We went straight to the Garden City County Jail. We were anxious to get there to see if Dick was all right. My thoughts fluctuated wildly. Secretly, I just knew or perhaps hoped that Dick would be able to tell us something that would give us some hope. Then, I would remember his recent actions and would feel deflated and fearful of what I was to learn while talking with my brother. Had the changes in my brother's personality caused him to kill four innocent people? The sick feeling I experienced the first moment I saw Dick in manacles and then listened to his ramblings remained in the pit of my stomach for months … actually for years.

The jail was not unusual in any way, at least not during the first day of our visit. The guards were calm and accommodating on that first day. Dick was seated in a small room with an unarmed guard standing watch over him. Dad and I were escorted into that small room. When I first saw the manacles, I thought: *"How could prison authorities think Dick could be so dangerous that he needed to be restrained? This was my big brother, the son who had in his early years been the golden boy for his parents. When all this is straightened out, the officials will apologize to Dick for treating him in such a manner."* But very soon I would come to know that Dick was in fact dangerous.

We sat in that small and claustrophobic room feeling totally out of place. I wanted to hug Dick, but I felt that was out of the question. Hugs just did not seem to fit in this setting, but I do remember patting Dick on the shoulder. I hoped that with this simple gesture, Dick would know that I cared for him very deeply and would support him through this ordeal.

I found it hard to say what I was thinking and feeling. A painful, hard lump formed in my throat as I watched Dad hug Dick with all the love of a father. His hug was firm and encompassing, even if it was a bit difficult to do while Dick wore manacles. Only a father could have managed a hug like that. The tears that filled Dad's eyes never fell, for Dad would not allow himself to cry in case that might weaken Dick's spirit. We had come to bring comfort and strength. After all, what else could we do?

Dick's body language vacillated. He acted like a lamb when pleading with us to believe his story. Yet, there was a cocky and almost arrogant flair at other times. I could not figure out if he was trying to give us courage that all this mess would be straightened out. There were other moments when he looked plain scared, as frightened as a little boy would be just knowing he was in trouble. These actions made it even more difficult to discern just exactly which statements of Dick's were true and which were fabricated.

After the strained greetings, we sat down, and after a brief silence, Dick spoke. He said, *"Dad, I know that I should not have been there. I just want you to know I had nothing to do with the actual killings. How is Mom doing?"* It was evident by the pained look on his face that he actually had some sense of compassion for the sorrow he was putting our mom through. It was unspoken that the reason she was not there was simply that she did not have the fortitude to withstand the visit to the jail.

I finally just blurted out, *"Dick, I know you could not have done this. I believe you. This has got to be some kind of mistake."* I only mouthed those words and wanted so baldy to believe them because he, my only brother, could not possibly be a murderer! The visit ended so quickly that I remember feeling disappointed. There were still so many unanswered questions. I left feeling no reassurance at all. Hopelessness filled me. I was beginning to understand just by being with my brother for that little while and listening to his confusing words that he might just be capable of the incomprehensible act of murder.

Dick talked to us like he was telling us about a TV show. I was astonished. Each detail seemed unbelievable. He kept saying that he just wanted to rob the Clutter home. How could a robbery turn into a bizarre event that captivated the attention of an entire nation? If robbery was the primary motive behind the crime, why was each family member bound in an inhuman manner? I wondered about those four people and whether they had pleaded for mercy or whether they struggled against the two intruders.

After seeing Dick, Dad and I located a motel room. We ate all our meals at local restaurants. It was during mealtimes that we quickly realized we were "an item" in this city. We received many strange looks and no welcomes. Our visit to the city actually made the local newspaper. I remember Dad asking, *"Dave, why would anyone be interested in us? We are not murderers, but just plain folk from Edgerton."*

Those reactions were a part of our being accused and convicted of the crime Dick committed. We were considered murderers. At least, that was how we felt. The people, the newspapers, and the jail employees did not have any clue about the kind of simple folk we were. They just knew we were related to the infamous accused murderer Richard Hickock. The people in the community were not openly hostile to us, but just curious. They followed us around. It was amazing how they just wanted to see us. We tried eating at different restaurants, but there were always people waiting and watching for us. The notoriety was uncomfortable and embarrassing.

The visit to the jail the next day was quite different from the first. Suddenly, all the jail employees had a different way of handling us. They were now all nervously packing guns. Each employee wore a sidearm or, if walking the halls, carried a shotgun. My dad was so shocked about the turn of events he looked over at me and said, *"Dave, you would think that we are here to try and break Dick out."* We learned again that day what the saying "guilt by association" really meant.

The employees at the jail were not exactly rude the second and third days of our visits, but the atmosphere had definitely changed. The wait to see Dick was much longer on the second day. The guard that stood watch in the small room in which we visited was now armed. The initial cordial greetings were now exchanged with formal and serious responses to any statements we made. The guards never threatened us in any way, but they were not as personable as they were during our first visit. I wondered what they might have been told that changed their manner of dealing with us.

It was during the second visit with Dick that he inquired about people back home. He earnestly asked: *"How is everyone holding up? What about my boys?"* His face reflected regret. I just had to believe that he was sorry for the pain he had caused our family. He could not have that deep and sincere look of grief on his face if he did not truly feel that way. Or could he? I sat in my brother's presence wondering how he could possibly be two people. Who was he … my penitent brother or my brother the murderer? I still wonder to this day what happened to Dick to change him so drastically and in such gigantic proportions that I, as his brother, sat before him with little recognition.

I was relieved to leave Garden City. Both Dad and I had trouble sleeping. I guess the fact that so many people thought we might also be violent criminals left us overwhelmed with negative emotions. Our drive home was longer and quieter, if one can imagine that, than the drive to Garden City. I do not recall my dad actually crying. Yet, his face was so pitiful; his face said so much about his pain. He locked that pain inside himself, and he never shared it with me. I doubt that he shared it with my mom upon our return home. He tried in earnest to be the strong one in this time of grief and sadness for our family.

Chapter Nine
One More Victim

Dad promised Dick he would do everything he could to help him. Our family attorney was a light-skinned black man named Miles Stephens, who had an office on Main Street in Kansas City. Mr. Stephens was a good man and had taken care of my dad's legal work when he purchased the farm. Dad and I took a day off from work for that visit in January 1960 to Mr. Stephens' office. Again, my poor mom remained at home, too distraught to come with us. More and more frequently she walked about our home doing her daily chores, speaking little, and crying often.

We drove in our usual silence to Kansas City. I had to do all the driving because my dad's pain from his illness, which had finally been diagnosed as intestinal cancer, had become unbearable. He could barely get around without someone assisting him. As I look back on that day, I remember the determined look of courage on Dad's face. He was trying everything he could to, as he put it, "*do Dick some good.*" I knew that my dad was eager to get to the attorney's office, but at the same time he was hesitant because he feared Mr. Stephens would not have any good news.

When we met with the attorney, Dad first asked him if he had any thoughts regarding a possible chance for some news "out of the blue" or a tidbit of information that had been overlooked that would or could be beneficial to Dick's case. Dad and I knew that with all the publicity about the murders any help for Dick would have to be something of a miracle. Dad was right on target about no miracles coming our way.

I remember sitting in the waiting room waiting for the appointment. The sun shone through the window warming our backs. Yet, our hearts were too burdened to enjoy the much-needed warmth on this very cold day. As Mr. Stephens greeted us with a cordial hello, I wondered if he would be the best defense attorney that my dad could afford. Dad and I knew nothing about public defenders, so we were earnest in our attempt to secure an attorney.

Mr. Stephens was a highly intelligent man who knew the score on life. This was the 1960s, the era of the civil rights movement, a time of deep, radical racial turmoil. Mr. Stephens warned us that as a man of color he might not be accepted in Holcomb. He was concerned and suggested that someone else might be better qualified to assist in Dick's defense. If my recollection is correct, he alluded to the fact that there had been talk that if Dad could pay a $100,000 fee, then perhaps he would be able to obtain a lawyer willing to work to clear Dick's name. Of course, as I sat in the leather chair in the attorney's office, I fully realized what a crazy notion that was. My family certainly did not have that kind of money, nor did we know anyone who did.

Mr. Stephens was very cautious in his conversations with us regarding Dick's guilt. He insisted that any assistance he could provide would only hamper Dick's case. He felt that the color of his skin would definitely put Dick's defense at a disadvantage. There were few blacks in Holcomb in those days. A black attorney in that town would be an oddity in itself and would draw more negative criticism to the case.

Fear crippled Mr. Stephens, as it did us. Just traveling through the rural area where we lived, my entire family was afraid of being killed as a retribution for the Clutter murders. The anger in Kansas as well as the entire nation about the killings was in large part due to the crystal-clean image of Mr. Herbert Clutter. He was the all-American father and husband. Who could possibly take anything away from such a righteous man? These facts humbled my family even more and made the shame so much greater.

After the appointment with Mr. Stephens, Dad was even more defeated. He just resolved himself to the fact that there was absolutely nothing he could do. It was mentioned to us that if a good lawyer could pin the murder charges on Perry Smith and only accessory charges on Dick, then Dick could possibly obtain a lighter sentence. We did not know how to go about the legal world to figure out how to do this.

As it turned out, the court appointed attorneys to defend my brother. The two men, if I remember correctly, were Arthur Fleming, who was to serve as Perry's lawyer, and Harrison Smith, who was to serve as Dick's lawyer. Later after appeals were filed, two other lawyers took the case. Their names were Joseph Jenkins and Robert Bingham. If these names are incorrect, it is because so many years have passed.

These court-appointed lawyers were just men, but they held our lives in the balance based on what they were capable of doing in their skillful attempt to be of assistance to Dick. I actually went to see Fleming and Smith after the first trial and I pleaded with them, saying if they knew of any other route, they should take it to help Dick. I look back at how naïve I was to think that a miracle might still occur. I did ask about the weapons that were used in the murders. There was a gun and a knife. The knife was Dad's, a beautiful homemade weapon. The gun, of course, was the one I had purchased for game hunting. The men told me that the two weapons would be returned to us. They never were, not to this day.

The consensus in newspaper articles and in general discussions around the country was that there was no need to spend tons of money imprisoning two worthless murderers. People wanted both men hanged! Only Truman Capote disagreed.

Capote spent a number of years writing a story about the Clutter murders that held both facts and fiction. I read that Capote thought by combining facts and fiction in his writing he contributed to a literary genre called the nonfiction novel. We do know that Capote interviewed both Dick and Perry, but more sessions were spent with Perry. We always wondered why this could be. What kind of fascination did the mind of Perry hold for Truman Capote? Perry was at least as guilty as my brother in murdering four innocent people … in cold blood.

Looking back on it now, I knew the outcome of the trial before I heard the verdict. I knew the ending to the story. I knew the sentence would be death, and I knew there was not a glimmer of hope for any good to come to my brother for his deeds. I knew it to be unthinkable that there would ever be another trial. I also knew in my mind and heart that there would be no success in hearings or appeals unless there could be some new evidence found. There was no new evidence to be found!

I did not attend the trial because I felt so helpless. For one thing, I could not miss work for two to three weeks. Another reason is that I just could not watch my parents as they were forced to sit through all the gory details of the crime. I also knew I had nothing to say. What more could be said? I wanted to believe my brother and every bit of the story he had shared with us. Yet, I knew the facts remained and pointed to his participation in the murders. I believed that the publicity about the crime had sealed his fate. No public sympathy existed for either of the two murderers. I was scared of the evil that continued to be directed at my family and me. I knew I was running away by my cowardly avoidance of the trial, but it was all I could do. The final verdict was murder in the first degree, punishable by death. Dick and Perry each received four counts.

My parents also knew in their hearts and in their minds that the end result would be the same no matter what happened. They feared that some angry citizens might "liquor up" and raid the jail just to get at my brother to kill him. They judged that the jail employees would not stop any such action. Fear can certainly cloud the way a person thinks.

We finally knew the fate of my brother. We knew he was doomed! I find it difficult to speak of the sadness that continued to invade our lives. The degree of emptiness was so devastating and it continued to grow to epidemic proportions. We shed many tears over the tragedy, not only for my brother, but also for the innocent Clutter family.

We went about our daily tasks without energy or enthusiasm. The pain that my dad suffered with his cancer paled in comparison to his mental anguish as he dealt with blow after blow in the aftermath of the crime.

The threatening phone calls never stopped. People screamed at us, calling us outrageous names and accusing us of being part of the vile crime. Occasionally, we shared with each other the hope that perhaps something positive would come out during the appeals process, but even as we spoke we knew it was only wishful thinking. The final verdict of murder in the first degree provided only more fear and no more wishful thinking.

I have read in recent years that disease is a result of problems or hurts not dealt with in life. My dad had been diagnosed with intestinal cancer prior to the murders. The doctors had told the family, but Mom did not want to tell Dad or speak to him about the seriousness of his disease. Looking back on it now, I do remember when Dad would have one of his attacks, he asked us what was wrong with him. Neither my mom nor I could tell him. The diagnosis of cancer back in the late 1950s was almost surely a death sentence. I now believe he knew he was dying, but could not discuss one more tragedy with the family.

I will always wonder if the events in the months that followed Dick's arrest made Dad's death come more quickly. He suffered to the point that he could not walk alone from the bed to the bathroom. His pain was the usual unbearable pain experienced by a cancer victim. I witnessed much of his suffering because I began staying at the farm as much as possible, trying to keep up with the work that Dad usually completed. His pain was heightened, I believe, by the turmoil in his mind as he tried to deal with the news coverage of the trial, the unfair treatment of our family, and the realization that his son was indeed a part of a high profile, gruesome murder. On June 20, 1960, seven months and five days after the Clutter murders, Dad died a broken man. He was riddled with excruciating pain as he lay in a bed of misery brought on by more than the cancer.

Chapter Ten
Dealing With Capote

How did Truman Capote write a book that combined fiction and nonfiction to create a nonfiction novel that remains prominent in American literature? Did he have any idea of the fame he would achieve after he wrote *In Cold Blood*? I have read that Capote's interest began when he read a short article about the murders that captured his attention. Shortly after that, Harper Lee, the well-known author of *To Kill a Mockingbird* and a childhood friend of Capote, traveled with Capote to Kansas to assist him in his efforts to write a book about the crime.

Capote arrived in Kansas during the investigation of the crimes. Capote conducted extensive research, interviewing many people as he tried to discover every angle of the crime. He even interviewed my parents. Mom and I were foolishly naïve because we thought by talking to Mr. Capote, he would work to find out the facts and write a book that might help Dick in some way. The outcome of his work was a nonfiction novel based on the details of the Clutter murders. *In Cold Blood* won acclaim in many literary circles and continues today to be considered a book that impacted the literary world in significant ways.

Capote contacted my mom about meeting with him at the Biltmore Hotel in Kansas City. I am almost sure that this was the name of the hotel. Time sometimes muddles the details. I remember Capote as a little, frail man. The first time I saw him, he was dressed simply in dark slacks and a regular, quite ordinary shirt. He introduced himself and politely shook our hands. He told us of his efforts in finding out everything he could about the crime and of his interest in putting all the facts into a book. He seemed confident in himself and in what he was doing. He shared that he was deeply sorry that we had to meet under these circumstances. His compassion was evident in his gentle conversation with us. We both liked him.

Capote's held three meetings with my mom in his hotel room. I never went to his room. I usually waited for Mom in the lobby. Mom would return to me with a blank look on her face, eyes red from all the crying. Answering questions about Dick continued to make her relive the horror of the crime. Mom returned to me after one of her interviews with Capote and angrily stated, *"Why did this have to happen to us and to my Dick? He is going to die. I cannot stop his death. I can do nothing to help him. Dave, what can we do?"* Her sorrow and agony tore holes in my heart. As usual, there was little I could say.

I realize now that Capote wanted to get "within" the heart of the sorrowful mother of a murderer. His questions left Mom drained, but by this time she was so empty. All hope was lost! These visits just added to the insanity of everything that had happened to her since her son participated in the crime.

In later months, probably latter March and April of 1960, I met with Capote when he spoke with my mom in the lobby of the Biltmore Hotel. We were always scheduled to meet at 10:00 am during those springtime sessions. It is strange now as I reflect on those visits. I remember that as a young man I kept thinking just maybe there was something this little, kind man could accomplish with his book. I knew how grave the matter was, but I guess that I was still looking for a better ending to my brother's story. Capote was the only person who ever tried to talk about the situation with us. I looked to his visits for some answers. I was too young and naïve to understand that he was merely writing a book and wanted all the facts. He was not a man with any power to change the course of events in our lives.

The part that Capote played in our emotional life was significant. I suppose he was brilliant in the sense of understanding the psychology of a person's mind. Once when he had walked Mom back to me in the lobby of the Biltmore, I heard him tell her: *"I understand that life has dealt a harsh blow to you and your family. Your family's pain will deepen as the time for the hangings comes nearer. Your sadness and sorrow would be what any mother would feel if put in the same circumstances."* Neither of us ever doubted his sincerity. He was genuinely concerned and openly expressed his empathy regarding our situation. His kindness was like a taste of cool well water on a scorching day.

As he bid us farewell, he told us in plain terms that he would give us monetary earnings for information. In fact, if my memory serves me correctly, he told me he was planning on dividing the proceeds of the book in three parts. My mom was to receive one third, I was to receive one third, and he was to keep one third. Of course, as time went by I wondered if I heard him correctly. Capote never gave Mom or me money. Capote did give Dick one thousand dollars, which Dick gave to Mom. No other money was paid. At the time, we were shocked that any money would be offered to us. The world was not as it is today. No one was trying to obtain our story for the *National Enquirer* or other tabloids. We just knew that we had met a man who was kind and sincere. He added the adjective generous to that description when he offered us money.

I have a recollection that Mom and her sister were contacted to go to New York City for a television show with Capote. Capote paid all the expenses, the airline tickets, hotels, meals, and such. Mom and her sister did not have that kind of money to travel all the way to New York City. All I remember is that Mom did have a chance to tell Capote at that time that the book had a negative affect on our lives. She was really devastated after the book was published. She honestly had thought Capote would be trying to tell all the truth. She had no idea he would do what any author would do. He wrote a book that was indeed about a sensational murder. His own subjectivity with all the details was woven into a book that would become a bestseller. How were we to know that?

I heard that many other people he interviewed were not happy about the way Capote portrayed them in the book. The descriptions of the people, our town, and even of my family were distorted, according to our way of thinking. We were just country folk who were thrown into a world we had no way of comprehending. I know for a fact that given her innocence Mom never would have talked to Capote had she known what he had in mind. Mom tried to tell him that her boy was not always bad. She still believed that he was basically good. I have no idea when that television show aired or on what station.

The book or television show never changed our lives in any positive way. From all the research I have done about the crime, I know that the book was not written with all the facts. I know that an author can do that with a book of fiction, and I also know that many other people were gravely affected by Capote's descriptions of them and their part in the crime, the investigations, and the outcome of the court proceedings. Many of the pages of the book contained statements that were not entirely true, at least as far as I can judge.

I remind myself that Capote capitalized on a sensational crime and then wrote a masterpiece, conjecturing on ideas that he deemed were notable and made the book more interesting. Indeed, it made the book interesting and it made him money. The persons left in the book's aftermath were wondering what people would think of them. After all, how were people in other states to ever know the truth of a person's character or the role a person played in the drama? Many people Capote interviewed felt much like my mother did, in that they felt exploited and deeply angry.

Capote claims he obtained the facts about my brother and Perry Smith through extensive interviews with them during their incarceration. I do know that he did try to learn everything he could possibly know about how they thought and what their motives were at the time of the crime. As I read the book, I was very shocked at some of the dialogue attributed to my brother. It spoke of a brother who was quite different from the brother that I knew. Dick's hidden desires and dark thoughts were disappointing and hurtful to read in print. The dark side of him depicted in the book was much darker than any of the changes I had noticed in his behavior prior to the murders.

I continue to this day to have conflicting feelings about Capote and his motive to write the book. He certainly was successful in his effort, but how much of the book is based on *all* of the facts? I understand that Capote was deeply sensitive and perhaps that colored his image of Dick, the people in our town, and the gruesome hangings that were the final result when the death sentences were carried out for both men. I now do understand that he intentionally wanted the book to be partially fiction, a nonfiction novel. Perhaps he just interpreted the information in order to fit his agenda for a bestseller. Who will ever know his true motive?

Chapter Eleven

Mom's Penitentiary Visits

After the conclusion of the trial, Perry Smith and Dick were sent to the Kansas State Penitentiary in Leavenworth County, Kansas. They arrived six weeks prior to the first scheduled execution date of May 13, 1960. In the conversations I had with him, my brother admitted to the wasted efforts at saving him. He saw no light at the end of the tunnel. He figured he knew what was to happen to him. He knew it was unthinkable that he would be allowed another trial.

I brought my mom to the penitentiary as often as was allowed prior to the hangings that finally occurred on April 14, 1965. During these drives she would say very little. My mom had always been an attractive woman with much to say. Her energy is what kept our family's home lively and organized. She changed so drastically! Without a church to turn to, with no friends to support her, and with her own relatives looking at her like she was some sort of freak, she withdrew into her own silent, sad world. She mentioned to me on a few occasions that she wondered if she and Dad could have done something differently.

I also thought that perhaps I could have done things differently. I remember even then not being able to talk about my own pain. My pain haunted me every moment of the day. I continued to ask myself why I had purchased that gun. I kept rationalizing to myself that after all the years of hunting all Dick wanted was a new gun. Who among us had the heaviest burden of guilt to carry? We questioned everything about our lives, our actions, and now every phone call we answered and every person we met on the streets. Questions with no answers marked our every breath!

My heart aches as I begin to tell the story of the penitentiary visits. As I have already said, my mom was a decent, churchgoing individual. The events that began on November 15, 1959, destroyed her world. Up to that moment in her life, my mom was so ordinary. She kept house, did laundry, and cooked for her family. She was far from being a pretentious person. She wanted nothing more than what she had. All she wanted was to serve the Lord and her family with gladness. Her favorite pastime was traveling with family members.

As I write this, I think it sounds so contrived. Yet, those who knew Eunice Hickock knew that she was sincere and very kind. I do not want others to think that she was unintelligent. She was a capable and organized individual. She knew that life could be more sophisticated, but she chose to keep her own life simple. Our visits to the penitentiary began in late March 1960 and were to continue until the final day of Dick's life. Mom's life would never be simple again.

My mom traveled to the penitentiary for five years with courage mustered from deep within her. I would always arrive at her house earlier than we planned to leave. I knew that she would be anxious about the trip and the visit to a destination that was stigmatized by society as socially unacceptable. I remember that we arranged to visit at least two or three times per month. What was she trying to accomplish with the visits? She had nothing to prove to society. She just wanted Dick to know that no matter what she would love and support him to the end.

The drive to the penitentiary was always on the same route. There were no interstate highways in those days. If I had to map the route today, I probably could not. I only remember that upon reaching Kansas City I would follow Highway 7 to Lansing. The trip was approximately thirty to forty miles; I don't remember the exact mileage. I do remember that Mom talked more than my dad did when we traveled to visit Dick during his initial days in jail.

Mom focused her conversation on questions about my job, general talk about the weather, and then she would voice her concerns for Dick's boys. She worried about how this crime was going to affect their lives. She wanted them to have a normal life, but she knew that it was too late for that to happen. Mom would often relive all the details of Dick's life, trying to understand his womanizing and his continual effort to raise money by writing bad checks. She really hated Dick's divorce from his first wife Carol. The 1950s and 1960s were a time when divorce was rare and socially unacceptable. Mom's old-fashioned values about marriage forced Dick to be very secretive about his second marriage. She heard he had fathered a child with his new wife, but we did not really see them often. We all later found out that Dick's second wife divorced him while he was in prison.

I remember the driveway going into the penitentiary. There was a guardhouse built at the entrance perhaps two or three stories tall that served as a watchtower for anyone entering the compound. We had to park our car and then enter. Upon entering, we had to state our names and see if we could get permission to go inside the building. It mattered not that we were on the visiting list. We still had to wait for permission to proceed.

I will never forget how the ordeal we endured just to see my brother played out. The main building was situated about fifty to seventy-five feet from the guard tower. We would enter a main door. In the initial visits, we were put in a small room on the left with a table to set us apart from my brother. There were guards all around. It was understood that we were not allowed to touch Dick. Not touching him was part of the rules for visiting prisoners. There were no glass walls to separate us.

I remember watching as Mom greeted Dick. I suppose all mothers would act the same way, though I do not really know. She was always trying in her own way to be courageous. She could not embrace Dick because that was not allowed. Her desire was to bring him hope, even though she knew there was none to be had! The room that we used for those initial visits was changed at some point. I suppose that the prison officials wanted to seclude my brother and us from others. It did not matter to us where we saw Dick. It was just important that we were able to see him. There was so little else we could do for him.

The first visit with Dick was very difficult. Mom could not help herself when she pleaded with Dick in asking the question, *"Why?"* Dick seemed to be emotionally flat as he spoke. He would say, *"Mom, I was just with the wrong person at the wrong time doing the wrong thing. I am so sorry that the events of that night have changed our lives. I worry so much. I worry all the time that my boys will be hurt by all this and their futures ruined."*

Only then would emotion overtake Dick and he would be moved to tears. *"Do you know what it feels like to know that I will not have a part in the future of my kids? I just hope Carol has found someone who will treat her right. I did not do right by Carol."* These were true words. As he sat in prison, he continued to be remorseful about his behavior during his first marriage. He often stated, *"I just wish I could go back and do it all over again."* We all knew it was too late for that.

Once, after listening to my brother lament his past, my mom quietly said on the way home, *"Carol is such a good woman. Why could Dick not have treated her right?"* Mom continued to search for answers, answers that she would never find. I wondered myself about his past actions toward Carol. There were times after he divorced her when I would hear him call her on the phone and purposely be mean to her. He was not providing any real child support and would insinuate that she could manage without his help. He lacked any respect for her.

Another penitentiary visit resulted in a discussion about the murders. As difficult as it was for my mom to discuss the murders, she managed the courage to ask, *"Dick, did you hurt any of those people?"* Dick sad and convincingly said: *"Mom, I don't know why that happened. Perry seemed to go crazy while we were at that house. He killed all of them. I would never hurt anyone."* Mom was so relieved she let out a gasp of relief and said, "That's what I wanted to know, because I always tried to teach you boys the right way." Dick further pleaded with Mom: *"I know I did a lot of things wrong, but I am not a killer. I am sorry for everything, but it is too late."* With tears trickling down Mom's cheeks, she lovingly told Dick, *"I love you and I will always think of you."*

At this point, I saw tears in Dick's eyes and he quickly put his head down. My heart was breaking at seeing my brother and my mom in such emotional turmoil. I prayed for God to help us if this awful fate was meant to be. I prayed for courage to face the tomorrows of our lives. I have to admit that I did ponder during these times the fact that my brother was perhaps just a good actor. Were his tears actually due to the fact that he continued to lie to his mother about the murders?

After this particular visit, we drove home in silence. When I dropped my mom off at her home, I got out of the car to hug her. When I got back in the car, I cried and cried. Never in my life had I felt so powerless to change a situation. I kept wondering if there was anything I could have done to help my brother be a better person. There was so much concern for my mom. My thoughts about my brother continued to focus on my disbelief that he could convince anyone, including his own mother, that he was an innocent man.

My mom continued to change. To say that she became remote is an understatement. I missed her so much even during our drives. The mom I knew was gone. Even today as I look at photos of her, I notice the inevitable change from a poised, beautiful woman to a woman who was overweight, sickly, and had great trouble with her nerves. Still, with all this turmoil, she refused to give up the visits to the penitentiary. She once told me that this was all she could do to make sure Dick was not lonely. Therefore, the visits continued.

Dick's moods ranged from confused to sane and from out of control to peaceful. Once, when experiencing one of his dark moods, Dick commented on how easy it would be to commit suicide. He had read a magazine about cutting the thick vein on the neck. He quickly said to my mom and me, *"Why would I go and do that, especially after all that I have done? I would not want our family to think that I was not man enough to walk to the gallows. No, suicide would make this whole thing worse than it already is."* These conversations were frightening, to say the least. We tried to talk some sense into my brother. Sometimes he calmed down, but at other times he remained distraught. I think my mom suffered the most through these emotional episodes.

The final visit to the penitentiary on April 14, 1965, is etched in my mind as if it were yesterday. I picked Mom up around 8:00 or 8:30 am. She was ready and waiting for me when I arrived. I knew she had cried all night because her eyes were red and swollen. She looked so awful, so pitiful. When I saw her, my heart broke, for I knew that she did not know how to deal with all the emotions she had been going through since the murders. Now, she had to face the hanging.

Even if this day was to put an end to the legal proceedings, the proceedings of the heart and mind were far from over. I remember thinking about how special her firstborn son was to her. She must have had so many dreams for Dick as she held him in her arms when he was a child. She watched him grow into a popular young man, and then watched him change into someone she did not recognize. I know she realized that this visit marked the last time she would see Dick. She had to be so frightened to know that by the end of the day he was to hang from a rope until dead. I gasped as that thought came to me. She looked at me strangely, but we could not speak for a number of miles.

After a long silence, Mom finally spoke. The words were the same ones she had spoken for months. She looked over at me with more tears streaming down her face and said, *"Dave, why do you think Dick did these things?"* I tried to console her and remind her that no one understood why Dick did such unthinkable things, but it was to no avail. She began to ramble.

"Dick was such a cute and adorable baby. He was always so good. As a child, he obeyed and listened to your dad and me. People who would see Dick would say what a pretty baby he was. Why he began smiling and being entertaining at four months old!"

My confusion and emotional pain began to intensify as I drove. In my heart and mind, I always knew that Dick was her favorite. Growing up, I had convinced myself that parents always prefer the firstborn. I told myself during those years that it was all right for them to love him more because he was their first child, but at that moment in the car I knew that I must have always been a bit jealous. Yet, I cannot begin to think that I could have competed with Dick for anything. He was more athletic than I was, seemed to obtain whatever it was he wanted, and almost always remained in the good graces of our parents.

I cried as I drove. I do not know if I was crying because I was once again facing the realization that my mom loved Dick more than me or that I was scared for my brother and what he was facing on this day. Or was I crying because I knew that after this day, I would never see my brother again? I also hated seeing Mom like this and I could do nothing to ease her pain. As I gripped the steering wheel, I prayed that God would help my mom.

I had no control over my emotions in dealing with my own pain. I looked at my petite mom and struggled to keep myself from falling apart. I did not know if I could be a source of strength to her in these final moments in the life of my brother. I never gave up trying, though. It had been so hard for all of us to just keep on living. Life does not stop when tragic things happen to families. At the time, it seems that everything should stop … at least long enough for a person to make some sense out of the confusion. The confusion had been going on in our lives for over five years. Over five years of fear, years of unanswered questions, years of cruelty from the public, and years of our own intense emotional pain.

The final visiting room was located deep in the prison at the end of a long hallway. We never quite figured out why this was, but I always thought it was because Dick was considered the worst of the worst of criminals. Then again, I thought maybe the guards wanted to give us more privacy for our final moments with Dick. Maybe they were shielding us, or themselves, from the spectacle of the entire situation. I never figured it out.

We traveled deeper into a world that was so foreign to us. We walked through a jail door that was opened from the inside. Once inside that small area, the gate would close behind us, while another opened in front of us. We walked with an escort about fifty to one hundred additional feet through the prison building. We then entered another locked door and met with Dick in a small room.

No guards observed our visit with my brother on that day. I guess they supposed that since there was no hope, the visits could only give some courage to my brother for his lonely walk to the gallows, where on that very night he would hang for his crimes.

Our visits were normally for a period of about one hour. As the execution date neared, our visits were lengthened. On this final day, we were allowed as much time as we wanted. I look back and think even the prison guards felt sympathy for my mom. However, this time was definitely without a doubt the most difficult visit. Our every step was slow and burdensome. The long walk to that small room left us with a feeling of deep exhaustion.

Upon leaving the prison that last day, Mom stopped in the parking lot and asked me yet another question. "Dave, do you think Dick is afraid?" I tried to help her, but I had to be honest. I said: *"I am sure he is afraid. Anyone would be afraid to face death in such a horrible way. God will be with Dick."* I was beginning to wonder about that, but it was all she and I had to hold on to that would give us some strength to live through this experience. I remember looking up at the sky and thinking, *"Lord, if you are up there, do something for us. I don't know what you can do at this point, but do something for us."*

Chapter Twelve
The Hangings

Our last visit with Dick began after we arrived on April 14, 1965, at midday. Mom was allowed to touch Dick all she wanted. She did this by hugging him often during those final minutes with him. I had never met Perry Smith, but I saw him sitting in a nearby room as we walked by. No other relatives were present to support us or to support Dick. We were alone in that cold and desolate place. We were there to say good-bye to my brother who was alive, but who would be dead within hours. I would never speak to my brother again. The pain was excruciating. The tears flowed from our eyes and the sadness within our hearts was an agony I had never known in my life. The pain is still as real to me now as it was on that dreary and sad day in April 1965.

One conversation that occurred that day was in reference to Dick's thoughts about dying. I really do not know if he was just trying to make us feel better, but he shared these words: "*The way I view this situation is that I would rather be put to death than spend the rest of my life in this place. Anyway, they say I am going to a better place.*" He had mentioned this to us before this particular day, but he seemed to need to say it again. Was he reassuring himself or us?

That day was different from any other day in which we had been present to visit with Dick. He seemed to be at peace with himself and the Lord. He knew the inevitable finality of his journey was going to take place that day and nothing was going to stop the events that would follow. As I looked at the resignation on his face, the same haunting questions came to my mind. Why did I not ask him about the remarks regarding "there will be no witnesses?" Why did I buy that gun? Why did I not realize that my brother had become unstable? Could I have stopped all of this madness? Could I have done anything to help by brother who had become a stranger to me? I knew that once Dick died, I would have no answers. Even at that time I knew I would never have a reprieve from my guilt.

A very strange incident happened in that last visit at some point and only for a fleeting moment before we left Dick. I saw a light of golden color around Dick's head. At first I just thought it was the lighting in the room. Later, on the way home, Mom mentioned that she saw the same thing. We both looked at each other surprised of such a thing. Now, I want to clearly state here that perhaps it was a lighting phenomenon. I will be the first to admit that by this point in Dick's life, there was nothing saintly about him. Yet, somehow, we needed to believe it was some kind of sign. We wanted to believe that the Lord was there to take care of Dick. We wanted to believe that Dick had asked forgiveness of the Lord. We wanted to know he was forgiven. I have no further explanation of that golden light that encircled his head, but to this day I still remember and see it clearly! We would not return later that evening for the executions. Surely, we thought that witnessing the executions would leave us more wounded than we already were.

Mom had been concerned about the details of Dick's burial. She asked prison officials about them while we were there for the last visit. Upon leaving the prison, she asked me to take her to Mount Muncie. She then let out a strange sound of grief and said, *"I cannot believe that I am here talking about where my son will be laid in the ground. God better help us!"*

My heart was pounding as if it was about to burst from my chest. I wanted to stop this madness and hold her in my arms. I wanted to scream, *"Mom, I am sorry. I am sorry for your pain. I am enraged at my brother for what he did. I am sorry that I am not your firstborn. I am sorry I bought the gun. I promise I will make it all better."* Of course, I did not say any of these words. I just listened. I just walked beside to the car and then drove her to Mount Muncie while both our hearts were breaking into a million pieces.

We drove slowly to that cemetery. We turned off the main street and followed a road from the main entrance. There was a bend in the road as I remember that was in close proximity to the spot where my brother would be buried. As I got out of the car and went to walk beside my mom, I had a thought that I must be dreaming. How in the world could my brother be dead in just a few hours? How could I know this fact and do nothing about it?

My mom was silent and her eyes were hollow. There was misery all over her face. She seemed to struggle to put one foot in front of the other. When we reached the grave site, she and I both fell to our knees. As I watched my mom, her tears would not stop. I could not console her, for no words could make any real difference. I cried with her.

The site was just dirt, plain ground. There was no headstone, but there was a plate that marked the spot for the burial of my brother and Perry Smith. I remember thinking, even though I understood the seriousness of Dick's involvement in the crime, how could Perry Smith, a detestable human being, lie next to my brother in the same cemetery? Now I realize that the state just buried them as a matter of fact. At the time, I thought this was awful. I wanted so badly to have a special place for my brother. I thought that if I could not help him in life, maybe in death I could find a better place. Why would he be connected to Perry Smith for eternity? I was still trying to hold on to the illusion that my brother was not as guilty as Perry. How awful a judgment of Perry is that? His family probably felt the same way about my brother.

We could not leave that place. We lingered around the grave site, looked at the scenery, and noted the peacefulness of the place. It was as if we were looking at a new place to live. Strange as it may sound, I think we both needed to know that Dick would have a good final resting place, safe from this world's scorn and perhaps even safe from himself. There had been so little else we could do for him. Before we finally left, Mom and I both touched the plate that signified the spot of burial. It was yet another way of touching Dick, an odd way of saying good-bye just one more time. After we completed this ritual, we were both eager to leave.

I later went back to that grave site after the burial to see if a headstone had been placed there. Upon leaving that second time, little did I know that I would be writing my story now many years later with a deep longing to travel the many miles back to this sad site to pay respects to my brother's memory.

As we drove home, Mom sobbed for the entire journey. The miles home were the longest and loneliest I had ever traveled. I had no words, I had no courage, and I had no strength. There were moments when I actually thought my heart would stop beating. I think I wished that it would, to rid me of my pain. I knew I would miss my brother, but I could not imagine the immense pain that my mom was dealing with in losing her firstborn child.

I drove Mom to her sister's home in Kansas City and then I drove to my home in Garnett. The rainy day heightened our pain. I remember thinking about Dick's body lying in the cold and wet ground. It gave me chills to think of my brother in this way. Many thought then and perhaps agree now that Dick deserved whatever punishment the legal system could levy on him. I only knew that my big brother was going to die and I was powerless to change any of the past or the future pain for my brother, my dear mom, or myself.

I went home to be with my wife, with a profound feeling of emptiness. I cannot name her, for she is like my children, whom I did not protect years ago. But I will do my best to protect them now. We were watching the news and heard the bulletin about Dick's upcoming hanging and the exact time it was to take place. I was feeling sick to my stomach and full of sorrow. To add to my misery, the phone rang and on the other end of the line was a person who yelled cruel things to me. I sat down and wondered how people could be so mean. My anguish was already so deep, so raw! I know I was bleeding inside my soul. I was being tortured. I wanted the entire ordeal to be over. Little did I know that night was only the beginning of a lifetime of pain, embarrassment, and cruelty.

The days following the hanging were some of the loneliest times of my life. Even my wife started to change in the manner in which she treated me. She began to openly express that Dick got what he deserved. While this may be true, it hurt then and it still hurts now. My belief was that family should stick together no matter what. I knew how she felt months before when a minister prayed that Dick would go to meet the Lord, and my wife openly expressed that he had no chance of seeing the face of the Lord. At a time when I needed to know that Dick would be okay in the afterlife, she reinforced doubt and uncertainty.

I cannot explain what happened to Dick in a spiritual sense. I just can tell you that I wanted him to be forgiven of his sins. I wanted him to rest in peace. All I can attest to is that when faced with something of this nature, unless one has been in this same type of predicament, one cannot possibly know how it feels when one has no hope for a loved one. The isolation I experienced after the executions was severe. I suppose some of it was self-imposed. My shame, guilt, anger, and bitterness began to rise within me. I never realized what drastic measures I would take in the course of my lifetime because of these unbridled emotions.

Carol, Dick's first wife, being the incredible woman she is, reached out to comfort Dick during his final hours before the hangings. I am thankful that she was able to be present with Dick on the night of the execution. One of Dick's last requests was that Carol would come to see him. Carol was married to her second husband at the time and her new husband willingly agreed to bring Carol to the penitentiary to fulfill Dick's request. They arrived on the night of the execution when Dick was to be eating his last meal. She remembers that he did not eat.

In speaking with Dick, Carol was surprised at his calmness on that evening. He acted as though he was going away on a trip. She said it was surreal to be standing next to a man who was to hang for his crimes and who was so totally calm. He told Carol and her new husband that he knew he was going to heaven. Carol was thankful that Dick was calm and assured. At the very least, she would be able to describe to her sons the manner in which their father faced his final hours.

Carol also vividly remembers her inability to cry that sad night. She felt the deepest pain she had ever felt, and her chest felt like a thousand elephants were standing on it, but she just could not shed one tear. She could not show any emotion. She could not cry even when Dick said, *"Tell my boys that I am so sorry about how everything came about. Also tell them I will be waiting for them in heaven."* She just stood patiently listening and wondering even then how a man could change so drastically and still be the same man. All of her boys were so young and she knew these events would change their lives forever. Yet, she stood stoically by Dick's side, listening to him talk.

Before Carol left the penitentiary, she said something to Dick and afterward wondered why she would have said such a thing. As Dick was groping to find some humor in the situation at hand, she laughingly said, *"Dick, if this was another state and you were to stand before a firing squad, you could be real smart and ask for a bulletproof vest as your last request."* To this day she thinks the stress and her emotional state must have spurred that comment. Looking back, she thinks the comment was inappropriate and quite silly. Dick only grinned slightly and then quickly spoke of other things.

Upon leaving the prison, Carol remembers how upset she was. Her upsetting feelings were not for Dick, but for the people he left in the wake of his actions … her boys, my mom, and me. She remembers thinking that capital punishment actually punishes the family of the criminal.

I can only be grateful that she was there for my brother on that dreadful night. She left the area of the prison where she and Dick spent those final moments, but not before remarking to her husband that she could see a golden aura around Dick's head. She knew as she stared at the light that it was real. She wondered about the meaning. She felt some reassurance that somehow Dick had made his peace with God. She still believed that he must have suffered permanent brain trauma from the car accident, and that it had adversely affected Dick's judgment and decision-making processes.

How many people would believe a convicted murderer could possibly have an aura about him? Three of us had noted this same aura during the course of the day and evening. It was not just a drop of bright color. It was just as we had seen in pictures of holy people. Dick was by far no saint. He was considered the worst of the worst at this time in history. I just remember, as Carol described, that Dick had a deep sense of calm and peace.

I kept thinking, *"How can he be that calm knowing that he would hang* for his crimes *in a matter of hours?"* I concluded that Dick must have made his peace with God. Nothing else could explain the peacefulness and the aura. I was thankful that Dick had realized his end was so near and he needed to know a forgiving God. I had nothing else to hold onto and holding onto that was better than holding onto fear.

As Carol was leaving the penitentiary, she remembers taking time to look into the eyes of her new husband, thanking him for being kind enough to bring her to the prison to bid farewell to the father of her sons. Her heart was as ours were, heavily burdened. Her only hope was that the aura was some kind of sign that meant Dick had found favor with God. Carol pondered the meaning of the last hours spent with her former husband, Dick Hickock, for many years.

Chapter Thirteen

Les, The Minister Present At The Hangings

Les was a longtime friend, brother-in-law, and minister for my brother during his final days before the execution. In 2006, he shared his reflections on my brother with my biographer. She has related her findings from Les to me, and together we have written about how this kind man of God was involved with Dick in a deeply significant way before his death sentence was carried out.

Les, a retired minister, has had time to reflect upon the events of his life. His connection with my brother is one part of his life that remains deeply branded into his mind and heart. Les first met my brother in Edgerton, where they shared a friendship and enjoyed hunting and fishing together. Les always liked my brother since they were close in age and enjoyed many of the same activities. Their friendship had grown over the years. They shared a brotherly companion relationship.

Les agrees with many others that changes in Dick's personality occurred after the automobile accident. He believes that the blow to Dick's head caused some type of permanent brain dysfunction. He found time and again that Dick's reactions were those of a person different from the man he had known. He believed that the doctors failed to ascertain the seriousness of the trauma to Dick's head during the accident. Dick went from being a nice friend to a stranger who began talking about all sorts of wild imaginative ideas. His ideas, of course, were all lies.

According to Les, the saddest thing was that Dick seemed to believe every incredible story he told. One bizarre story that Dick shared with Les was that he had to carry an atomic bomb across town. There were many more such stories that went beyond an average person's thinking or rationalizing. Knowing that Les, a reputable minister, saw these dramatic changes in Dick has helped me to understand that the man involved in the murders associated with *In Cold Blood* was a man who was definitely a stranger. More importantly, he was a man who was mentally ill and perhaps criminally insane. I knew Dick's conversations bordered on being unstable, but at the time I did not realize other people could see the vast difference in Dick and his behavior after the accident.

No one could have been more shocked than Les when he heard that my brother was part of the Clutter murders. His friend had changed, but he had no idea that his mind had shifted so negatively and drastically that he could have committed or participated in a crime of this nature. Les said that he just could not give up on Dick. He stood by their bond of friendship knowing that the Lord's work could not stop. It mattered not that his friend was convicted of murder. He visited him often at the penitentiary. Chaplain Post, the penitentiary chaplain, accommodated Les and allowed him to visit and even share meals with Dick. I am so grateful to know this. My mom and I had worried so much about Dick's mental state, his loneliness, and whether he would repent and find peace with God before he died.

Les recalled the first time he saw Dick in prison. He entered a blockhouse that had a table. Dick sat on one side of the table, and Les sat on the other side. There were no screens to separate the criminal from his visitor. The guards left them alone. The visits continued throughout Dick's incarceration. Les recalls visiting at least fifty times or so. Again, I am grateful that Dick had some spiritual direction and a friend. I know I was not much help. Even knowing this fact so much later in this story and in my life gives me some consolation.

One of the most remarkable visits Les had was one in which Dick announced that he had been "saved." Les questioned him since he had been trying to help Dick get right with God, but had not succeeded. I believe the seeds Les planted in Dick's mind allowed Dick the understanding of what it meant to be saved and the importance of getting right with God before his execution. How exactly did Dick find salvation? One of the chaplains from the prison brought a minister to see Dick. He said that the minister had driven from Texas for three hundred miles in an old beat-up car just to talk with him. This minister was allowed to see my brother.

The minister said, *"Son, God sent me here to say he loves you."* Dick immediately started to cry. Les had told him that he needed to get right with God. At that particular moment, Dick, knowing he had no hope of ever living a normal life, knowing he was to die in the near future, fully realized the graveness of his predicament and accepted Jesus Christ into his life. When Les visited Dick a few days later, Dick told him he had "gotten right with God". Les stated that he was more than elated to know that the power of his Lord was now going to be with his friend during his final days. I was so relieved when I was informed of these details. There had been talk with Carol about Dick's final attempt to make peace with the God he had turned away from, but the intimate details came only during the writing of this book. We had hoped for as much, but Les's story gave me confirmation.

There was calmness to Dick after his acceptance of the Lord into his life, according to Les. He even sketched a picture of Christ that he gave to Les as a gift. He signed it simply Hickock. Les told me there were those who wanted to give Perry Smith credit for the drawing. Les knew better, for he had been involved with Dick for months and knew of his work on the sketch. The likeness to Christ was present to each viewer of the sketch. I wonder if maybe both men had repented and both sketched Jesus as they saw him. Will we ever know?

On the evening of the execution, Les's wife begged him not to attend the hangings. She told him that once Dick died his pain and suffering would be over, but that Les's suffering for his friend would continue. No truer words could have been spoken. Les went to spend Dick's final hours with him. He was with the prison chaplains as they tried to reassure Dick.

When Dick was given his final meal of fried shrimp and a dessert of ice cream with strawberries, which he could not eat, he asked Les and the other chaplains if they wanted his meal. All said no. It was a strange and tense wait. For one thing the clock would tick right before the minute hand would move. Of course, everyone was watching the clock. It was eerie to know that in just a few hours, and then minutes, Dick's life would be over.

The conversation centered on talk about heaven. Les told Dick since he had turned his life over to Christ, he would see the face of Jesus. The other pastors contributed to the conversation, relating their belief in the forgiveness and loving care of the heavenly Father. All the same, the sadness was quite overwhelming. As the time grew nearer and the inevitable was to happen, the guards came for Dick. Les could not go with him to the gallows. It was just too difficult to watch him die.

Dick took a final look at his friend as he pointed up to heaven and said, *"See you up there, Les."* Les's sorrow was naturally filled with compassion and empathy. He knew that Dick's remark was in reference to the following scripture from John 14:6: *"I am the way, the truth, the life: No man cometh unto the Father, but by me."* Les had shared this scripture many times in his own efforts to explain the significance of Jesus to Dick. He knew that at that moment, without a doubt, Dick had repented and was looking to the heavens for help.

Les remembers Dick's final smile and his last words. When the final moment arrived for the hanging of the two men, Perry made the comment, *"This is a helluva way to die."* Dick said something to this effect: *"I hold nothing against anyone. I should have tried to stop all of this. I deserve this. I am going to a better place."* After the hangings, the grave master asked Les if he wanted to make a final farewell to his friend by viewing the corpse. Les refused. The grave master tried to convince Les and told him that he wished he would. When Les asked why, the grave master became insistent, saying, *"Strangest* thing. *Smith died with a scowl on his face, while Hickcock died with a smile."* Just knowing this made Les understand, once again, that Dick had truly made peace with God.

Les also saw a phenomenon occur that evening. He, too, saw an aura, a glowing effect that surrounded my brother in those final hours. Mom and I had seen the same aura earlier that day. Carol had noted it! Les just had to believe that Dick had found salvation in those final days before his death. As a man of God, it was his only explanation for what he knows was not his imagination. Les was a bit baffled as he tried to make sense of who was really guilty, his longtime friend Dick, Perry Smith, the short, dark stranger from Nevada, or both misguided men?

Les knew that Perry Smith had done at least one decent thing in his lifetime. According to Les, Perry admitted that he had committed all the murders. Les begged the Governor of Kansas to commute Dick's sentence, but it was to no avail. Les believed that because the governor had run for office at a time when Kansas was so fearful of the crime and its aftermath, he had to "Hang those boys." Les knew, as we all did, that the murders frightened many people in Kansas. Everyone wanted the two "boys" to be put to death. Perhaps then Kansas's citizens would be free from their fears. We all understood that. It was so genuine and indicative of Les's loyalty to try just one more last attempt to get some assistance for my brother.

Les returned to his church where he was pastor, struggling with his grief. His church council noted his extreme sadness and his overwhelming pain. They offered him time away from his duties. A deacon of the church took him fishing. It was during this time that Les was able to put the pieces of the puzzle together. He realized he was relieved and his heart was gladdened to know that Dick had accepted Jesus Christ as his forgiving Savior prior to the execution. He came to know that perhaps the primary purpose of his friendship with Dick was just to be a helper in his time of need. Although it has taken many years to fully come to terms with the seriousness and tragedy surrounding the Clutter murders and Dick's part in them, Les still has emotional moments when he reflects on the events relating to his longtime friend, Dick Hickock.

Les had planned to write a book of his own. It was to be entitled *Under the Blood* and was to have explained the "other side of Dick Hickock." He thought he would tell of the beauty in Dick as a person. He wanted the truth to be known that although Dick was involved in the Clutter murders, there were many grave misconceptions about him, his personality, and the entire sequence of events as reported in the media. He asked Carol, Dick's first wife, if she would mind if he wrote the story. Carol had remarried and was trying to get her life and the lives of her children back to normal. She was not in favor of Les's efforts to write such a book. Thus, Les gave up on the idea of telling the "other side of the story."

Knowing about Les's relationship with Dick does help me find peace in knowing that my brother did in fact turn to the Lord. So many times I wanted to believe this fact, but I was not so spiritual myself. I thank God that Les could do what my family and I were not capable of doing. He was the best friend my brother could have possibly had and he led Dick to a peaceful and holy death. Perhaps many would say there could be nothing holy about Dick Hickock. Holiness comes from the One who creates us. Who are we to judge?

Richard "Dick" Hickock as a young boy

Richard "Dick" Hickock holding his brother Walter David Hickock

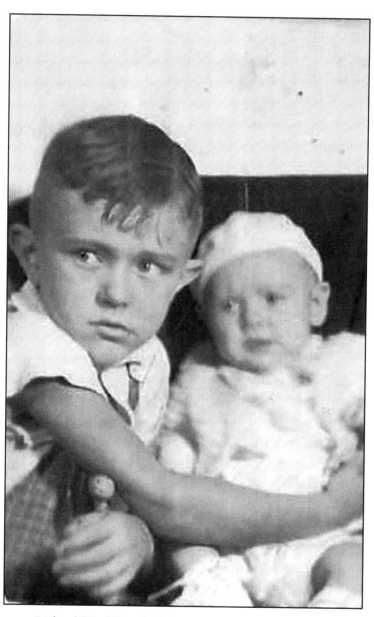

Richard "Dick" Hickock holding Walter David Hickock

Eunice Hickock, mother, holding Walter David Hickock

Walter Samuel Hickock, father

Hickock Farmhouse in Edgerton, Kansas

Walter David Hickock, Richard "Dick"
Hickock's first wife Carol & Dick
Hickocks with fish caught in the stream on the Hickock farm (1956)

Richard "Dick" Hickock as a young man

1949 high school photo of Richard "Dick" Hickock

Walter David Hickock and his last wife Rosita (1984)

PART II
Walter David Hickock

Chapter Fourteen
Running Scared

I went about my everyday life after the hangings took place. I tried to be a normal person. I really had forgotten what it was like to have a normal life. I remained so ashamed of my brother. I went through much self-doubt. I continued to fear that I shared my brother's cold blood. I looked away from people as I walked the streets of the city where I lived. I played mind games in my head, always wondering what people might be saying about my family and me. My emotions ran wild and crazy. There were times when I would feel numb inside and I would not allow anything to touch my emotions. I hardly slept. Peaceful rest just would not come. I believed people hated me and would condemn me all of my life. Absolutely no one knew what I was dealing with in my head!

In 1966, when the notoriety of the crime became more than a constant struggle and embarrassment, I did the unthinkable and ran away from the people who loved me. I made it look like it was the right thing to do, but it was so wrong to run. It started me on a pattern of running that would last for the next thirty plus years. I was seeking peace that would be a long time in coming.

I quit my job and left my wife and my four children to travel about the country as a water tower technician. I boarded a bus in Kansas City for the first bus ride in my life to travel to Philadelphia, Pennsylvania. My newly found job provided my travel and work. I would work for three to four months, returning home periodically with my boss to spend two or three days visiting my family.

The hurtful and embarrassing fact now is how I could leave my four children. My own problems loomed larger in my head than my need to be a good father. I look back and cannot believe that those four beautiful children were not reason enough to keep me in Kansas. I realize now that I was running away from Dick's crime and the total devastation that it had brought upon my family and me. Even the fact that my dad had passed away and left my mom a grieving widow did not keep me in Kansas. My mother and her sadness weighed heavily on my heart, but I had no way to help her. The selfishness of my actions can only be explained in that my mind was overwhelmed with confusion. The fact remains, though, that I was selfish. I rationalized my leaving by saying that I would be back and I would be making more money. I knew then and still know that I was running as far away as I possibly could from the maddening reality.

It was because of my absence that my wife became angry. Or perhaps it was because she had been left to deal with the aftermath of the crime and the never-ending talk about it. I began to realize that Dick's actions haunted her. She openly discussed Dick's guilt. She never liked Dick and his unthinkable crimes gave her a chance to verbally express her disgust.

I saw a change in her affections toward me. My visits home were very painful and once again I felt betrayed. I realized that I probably deserved her wrath. How could a man leave a wife and four children? All the reasons I gave are mere excuses. I used the job as a tool to get me out of Kansas. I felt very guilty, but it did not stop my escapades. Instead, I traveled more extensively throughout the states, working wherever I was sent. I enjoyed moving about from place to place. The 1960s were a fairly innocent time. People were usually welcoming in each town. If I was lucky, no one asked me my name. If they did ask and did not associate the Hickock name with the Clutter murders when I told them, I was always relieved.

More times than not, however, the people in these areas, upon hearing my name, would make the association to the Clutter murders and the welcome mat would be jerked away! It is important to note at this time that the newspapers throughout the country continued to write articles about the Clutter murders. People in even the smallest towns knew about them. There was no place to escape. If a link was made with the Hickock name, I was asked of my association or kinship with Richard Hickock.

I continued in my job of painting water towers (taking one to two weeks to complete each job), traveling from Pennsylvania, Georgia, West Virginia, Florida, and returning to Pennsylvania. My spirit began to grow more troubled during my work travels. I had abandoned my wife and I knew I was losing her. I was never sure if my wife grew lonely from the lack of my being home or if she just hated being associated with the Hickock family.

Whatever happened caused her disillusionment and led her to a life of partying while I traveled in my efforts to make a living for the family. I sent money home from time to time, trying to support my children. I understand that I was a delinquent husband and father. At a time when they all needed me, I let my own problems keep me running. Of course, wisdom does not always come to us when we are young. When I realized what my wife was doing with her life, I tried to be free of that pain by living the wild life myself.

My own disillusionment made it so easy for me to rationalize my "evening life." There were some people in each town that were entranced by the work we did at painting the water towers. Think about it! The daredevils we must have looked like as we hung from a rope cleaning and painting water towers. Some people in each town seemed to be enthralled with our dangerous business. I recall the life of moving from town to town, and enjoying the bar scene and meeting a variety of women who thought I was dangerously exciting well into the late 1960s. Of course, this life led to the loss of my wife. Since we had not formally been married, there was no divorce. She did obtain a judgment for non-support and abandonment.

I was more than happy not to have any reason to go back to Kansas. The memories entrenched within my spirit haunted me even more when I was in Kansas. I would forget Kansas as I enjoyed the company of a variety of women in my travels. I especially appreciated each short period of time with new friends before they would connect my name with the Clutter murders. Depression became a constant companion. Thoughts of suicide monopolized my thinking, for I thought suicide would be a welcome relief. I started hiding behind a mask each day, pretending to be a happy-go-lucky guy!

There were so many times when I thought about doing something really drastic, like committing suicide. I went out in my car numerous times to deliberately drive on roads surrounded by big ditches, such as on Interstate 35. I would speed up to eighty or ninety miles per hour and think about driving my car into a ditch just to make sure I would kill myself on impact. The one question I always had in my mind was who would really miss me? I was a Hickock, the brother of the infamous murderer.

Other times, while I was working as a water tower technician, I would think that if I tied a rope around my neck and jumped off the 120- to 150-foot towers I would be out of my misery in almost an instant. I even thought about driving to the busiest intersections and steering my car into the first vehicle that came my way. Then, I would shockingly remind myself that I was no better than my brother. I would become saddened at the thought of harming an innocent victim. I would be angry with myself when I would think that I could make a victim's loved ones suffer. How much like my brother would I be then?

The thoughts of self-destruction continued to haunt me. After driving toward my own suicide attempts and then driving to wherever I was staying, I would always become even more despondent. I thought about slitting my wrists. I knew that I would lose blood and slip away from life quietly and simply. I did not realize that I was what psychologists would call today clinically depressed. I just thought I was worthless. I would return to my hotel and sit in my darkened room in complete silence, crying tears of mixed emotions. A part of me was usually glad that I had some sense and that I arrived at the hotel unharmed. A part of me cried because I was not brave enough to end my misery, once again confirming the depths of my cowardice.

My emotions stayed at such highs and lows. A few days after these episodes, I would ask myself why I had not just gone through with the plan. I really wondered if I had anything to lose. I believed that I had lost everything. I really missed the family I had before the murders. I would think of my children and think of how they would feel if they read about my suicide in the newspaper. I know that I still cringe when I see material written about my brother or the Clutter murders.

Why did I not go through with suicide? Amazingly, I had no one to talk me out of it. The only thing that I feared when I planned my suicide was that I would fail and end up in a vegetative state. I worried that if that happened, I would become a burden to others. My children did play a part in my walking away from suicide. Why would I make them wonder about my motives? I was so reckless in my life; I suppose I am lucky to be alive to tell my story.

So, instead of suicide I just decided to keep running. I even had the strange notion that leaving would help my children in some way, protecting them from hurt and shame. Strangely, as I now look back, I realize that it was not Kansas that was troubling me. It was my own state of mind. I realize now that what I needed then was some type of counseling. Back in the 1960s, people did not talk about healthy self-esteem or obtaining counseling to cope with life's experiences. I had no understanding of the world of psychiatry or psychology. I was dealing with the normal stressors of marital problems, concerns about the children, and the added turmoil of the constant reminders of the crime. I did what I had to do or thought I had to do.

Besides the thoughts of suicides, there were numerous incidents in which my life could have been taken from me. I once fell inside a water tower in Florence, South Carolina, as our crew was cleaning. I had to have 159 stitches on the front and right side of my head. My collarbone, which was broken in two places, was wrapped to hold it in place until surgery could be performed. On this hospital visit I remained bed-ridden for two weeks. The time spent in that hospital bed began my wondering as to why the Lord was keeping me alive. I could have died in that tower from the blunt blow of the fall or the other injuries, but I did not. I believed in my heart I was not worthy to stay alive.

At age thirty in 1967, I met a lovely woman, strangely enough, through my first wife's brother. On one of my rare visits to Kansas, we had a brief encounter of three or four days before I returned to work. She did know that I was going to Wheeling, West Virginia. I was not surprised that within a few weeks she arrived by bus with her toddler in hand and moved into the hotel with me. I was happy to see her since we had a good rapport with one another. She was just happy to have a boyfriend with money. I had money, but little else to bring into the relationship. I was still so scarred by my past experiences. We married in Cal, Missouri, and later moved to Tipton, Missouri, to live near her relatives. I left the water tower business in order to settle down with her and we brought another child into this world. I supported four of us by working in a bar.

Later, I returned to Kansas City to search for employment opportunities. Finally, the publicity surrounding the Clutter murders had begun to wane. I mistakenly thought that people had forgotten the awful crime. The difficult task of finding a job began. When applying for jobs, the notoriety of the murders and the Hickock name closed many doors for me. Some potential employers would not interview me, some lied and told me there were no jobs available, and some were afraid to even look my way.

No one in Kansas wanted any association with the Hickock name! The very sound of the name frightened people. I was once again confronted with the anger and the continued fear left in the aftermath of the horrendous crime. I fought all the same feelings I had in my earlier life when I just ran away. My own fear, paranoia, shame, and grief resurfaced. I remember thinking and wondering if I ever was going to get away from the Hickock stigma. Was I ever going to be normal again?

I remember applying for a job at a trucking company in Kansas City, Missouri. The ad had just appeared in the paper and I quickly went to apply. I wanted to make sure that I could provide for my new family and I did not want to repeat the mistakes I had made with my first family. I just wanted to make better choices for my second family. At this point, I had no communication with my first family because all contact with me had been severed.

I just had to make this job work. When I first arrived at the trucking firm, the interviewer was very interested in me. I know he saw my determination to get a job and my enthusiasm about finding work. He lost his interest when the Hickock name was mentioned. The interviewer acted as though his memory had failed him. He remembered the job opening had been filled. The pain of the continued rejection began to grow inside me like a cancer. I was angry by this stage in my life. I was angry about many things. I did not have a killer mentality. I did not have an inkling into the reason my brother had committed such violent acts. He had been hung for his misdeeds. Why was I to suffer for this for the rest of my days?

Finally, I did secure work with the Missouri River Barge Line Company. I was thrilled to have a job that would require me to move around. Kansas did not want me. I was an unwanted person. I was always treated with fearfulness and an attitude of "let's get him out of here." My work involved pushing barges loaded with grain in the summer from Kansas along the Missouri River, and in the winter when the Missouri river froze, we traveled along the Ohio River to Pittsburgh, Pennsylvania, to Chicago, Illinois, and to New Orleans, Louisiana, via the Mississippi River.

I was expected to live on the boat, as room and board were provided. I began to thrive on these living arrangements. They allowed me the opportunity to work, but continually kept me moving away from any people who might know of my history. This was an answer to my need. I could support my family, not return to Kansas except for brief visits, and never get so closely involved with people that they would know I was a Hickock.

My new relationship with my second wife grew stale. I believe she had grown weary of the emptiness of her relationship with me. She did not understand my need for complete isolation from people. She did not understand the demons that haunted me on the streets of Kansas. She did not comprehend my paranoia. She just knew that she was alone most of the time raising our children.

I had become the absent husband and father again. Even as I knew this, I could not change my attitude that I finally deserved to be happy. I knew that my existence was merely that, an existence. I just wanted to survive every day and rid myself of the growing insecurity. I had not figured out the answers to all that had happened. I had not determined why I should be shunned by a society that did not have any clue as to who I was. It is easy to understand why my wife began to see other men. On the occasions when I came home for one of my brief visits, she would inform me of her escapades. She would always be brutally honest with me.

Of course, with my low self-esteem, I believed I deserved what she was doing. I was leaving her alone and not taking much care and concern with her or my children. I never reassured her of how much I loved her. I was repeating my mistakes. I now know that if we do not love ourselves, we tend to be unable to love others. This lack of self-esteem and my inability to communicate my feelings is what continued to destroy my relationships. I tolerated such actions because even though I was not the best husband and father, I wanted to save my marriage. I longed for the security of a wife and a home, and I wanted someone to love me unconditionally.

A major part of my problem was that I had no skills in expressing my own needs and concerns. By running and avoiding discussions, I only built more confusion and unrest within my family and myself. I realized that my wife grew weary of the distance I kept between us based on the "story" that I kept locked within me. Eventually, I paid Miles Stevens, our family's longtime lawyer, $350 for a divorce.

I remember my final hours with my second wife, hours filled with mixed emotions. I was angry with her, angry with myself, confused as to what went wrong, and relieved that I could just run away and hide myself in my work. She brought me to the airport, sharing a casual good-bye. She also stated that she was on her way to her boyfriend's house. The final remark hurt me deeply. Once again, I believed with all my heart that I deserved this treatment and that I deserved the pain. I still wonder if I could have saved that relationship. Did my lack of caring for her push her into the arms of other men? I know I provided a living for her and the children. Yet,

I provided little emotional closeness. I could not remain committed to anyone, including myself. I realize she needed so much more than I was capable of giving her.

My next job brought me to the city of Uncle Sam, Louisiana, where I found work on boats hauling grain up and down the Mississippi River. The boats once again afforded me the freedom of being constantly on the move. The water served as a medium on which I could flow away from the troubles and demons in my mind. I felt set free every time the boat left a port. On my first job on these boats, there was a worker who was studying criminology at Louisiana State University who instantly recognized the Hickock name. This news spread quickly throughout the company. Many questions remained and were asked occasionally, but the response in this situation was less negative than it was in previous jobs. I do not know if it was the location or just that some time had passed; my days were not as haunted as they were before.

Once, when working on the boats, a fuel line broke, resulting in my left foot being broken, but I was stubborn and continued going to work on crutches. I was not trying to be brave. I needed the money, so I had to work. Yet another injury occurred when I got caught between a fender and the side of a boat. My left arm was paralyzed. Surgery was performed on my neck to free the spinal cord injury and restore movement to my arm. At another time, I caught a falling object and the blow resulted in my right wrist being crushed. It took three surgeries to repair my wrist. I never regained flexibility of movement.

There were other injuries that could have been fatal. Was I just being fatalistic with my life? Was I trying to end it all? I still wonder about that today. Now that I am older, I have heard that some people are on self-destructive patterns in their lives. Was I? I continued to question why God would spare my life. Why me? I am what I hear about in church. I am an unworthy servant. I knew I should not question God, but my painful memories would never leave me.

The guys that worked with me thought I was jinxed in some way. I hate pain. I did not try to get hurt. I wonder today that perhaps in my own way I just did not care, and was careless just to end my suffering. There was a constant battlefield in my mind and the battle cry was always the same. The cry assured me that I was nothing.

I only know that by running I abandoned my mom, my children, and every woman who loved me. I spent time at a variety of jobs in different cities across the United States. I did not care where I worked or lived as long as it was not in Kansas. What was going through my mind during those days of constantly running from the truth? I was just an ordinary guy trying to survive, and my mind did not grasp a way to cope with the constant reminders of the murders.

I had watched many people hit snags in life and yet manage to work out the kinks and keep on enjoying life. I could not do that. I was not a well educated man, having only a high school diploma. I could read and write, but I did not have any other skills that would have helped me cope with the situations following the murders. The reminders were constant and came at surprising times. I wanted to believe that once some time had passed, the constant talk about the murders would die down. When I thought I was safe, something would happen to remind me of my past.

In 1972 or 1973, I met my third wife in a hotel lounge in Port Arthur, Texas. She was fifteen years younger than me and had two children. I lived with her for quite some time before marrying her. The union was short-lived. My feet were itchy to move out west to Wyoming and she was not enthusiastic about going. When I approached owners of large ranches in my search for a job, the usual questions arose, such as where I was from and what my previous employment experiences were. I was surprised to find that these "cowboys" knew the Hickock name and were inquisitive to know all the gory details. It only took one person to start talking and the cycle of rejection and isolation would begin anew. One ranch owner, when finding out the details of my background, quickly released me from my job. He did not want anyone of my caliber associated with his ranch, his family, or other employees. I was some kind of evil threat.

I secured a better job making more money at Exxon in a uranium mine in Douglas, Wyoming. It lasted only one year and I believe that I was let go as soon as the management realized who I was.

I returned to the south, working briefly in Galveston, Texas. My next move took me to Morgan City, Louisiana, where I worked as a superintendent of Conrad Industries building barges.

My third wife told me she was tired of being associated with the murders. She, too, had instant notoriety wherever she went and she believed there would never be an end to the madness of the murders. She left me and moved to Galveston, Texas. Another relationship failed. I just could not seem to hold a family together. I remember wondering if I was as "bad" as my brother. Why could I not love and be loved?

Looking back on my relationships with women, I think my third was the one I truly missed. I often wished I could have had that woman back in my life. I probably loved her more than any of my wives. Yet, I never knew how to talk to her about situations or emotions that were continually being revived each time I tried moving to another location. I never told anyone that once the murders and the hangings were behind me, my entire life had been one of running scared. I was never accepted because I had been branded a murderer even though I had never pulled the trigger! I tolerated being ostracized by moving to another city. Little did I understand that with each rejection I continued to have my self-esteem ripped apart.

My final move was to Jennings, Louisiana, where I worked as a bartender and later as a greeter at Wal-Mart. Every day I greeted hundreds of people who were willing to accept my smile and my cheery hellos. This simple job provided acceptance, a way to be no one and someone at the same time. I finally began to let go of the fear I had of anyone knowing me. I found joy in my work, work that I continue to perform to this day. I always did love people, and my parents raised me to respect people. In my simple way of greeting, handing shopping baskets to people, and in being a reliable employee, I have found a place where I am comfortable. It may not seem like the ultimate of jobs to most folks, but, to me, it is a community of acceptance. The people within Wal-Mart and within this average Louisiana town have helped me begin to release some of the pain.

I am a much older man these days. All men in their latter years, I suppose, look back on their lives and try to understand that they did the very best they could in their lives. I cannot say that I did the best that I possibly could. On many days, I even wonder why I am still alive. There were so many times during the trauma of the days following the murders, the wearisome days of the trial, the day of the execution, and the empty life left in the aftermath of the events, in which I would have just done anything to stop the pain.

Just after the premier of the movie *Capote*, I relived every day of 1959 up to the present over and over again in my mind. Wondering, always wondering! What could have changed the horrific times I have lived through? This burden of guilt that I try to deal with, pray about, and reflect upon for some semblance of order comes back lashing his ugly tail. Will it ever stop? I fear it will not. People tell me that I need to pray that God will heal me. Am I worthy of that healing?

I could have better loved the women in my life and my children. No wife or child deserves what I dished out. I did not provide for them in the proper manner. I waited years and years before I even tried to contact them. It is no wonder that they do not really want to have anything to do with me. The men that were there for them are their real fathers. I can barely speak these words, but I was a cowardly imposter. How deeply I realize that these words are true. I do not look for pity, for I do not deserve it. My running was part of the immature and fearful boy who grew to be a fearful and insecure man.

As I continued in my life, I added more blame to my conscience. With all the traveling I did with my jobs and the running I did in the aftermath of the murders, I also stopped going to see my mom. In my mind, I thought that Dick had been her favorite child. He was so special in her eyes. Can anyone be jealous of a dead man? I was, or perhaps I was jealous of his memory. I had to distance myself from Kansas. The inner blame I held for purchasing the gun and for spending a lifetime on the run haunted me then and continues to haunt me now. It follows me every day of my life.

What could I have done differently? I could have stayed to help my mom through her grief. I could have stayed with the women in my life and better cared for my children. How I wish I had been more attuned to the needs of my mom, my wives, and my children. How I wish I could have had the skills to help them cope. How I wish that I had learned to face reality and move on to a more productive life. I was a coward and I just did not know what else to do. I do not often judge others today about cowardice because I know the burden that has weighed heavily on me all these many years. It was unacceptable to walk away from reality to ease my pain. When I think of the unspeakable hurt I put my loved ones through, I am humbled beyond words.

Chapter Fifteen
Rosita

My rescue came from a strong and energetic woman named Rosita. My relationship with her was to be my fourth and final one. I promised I would make this one work. I guess all people remember meeting a soul mate, the blossoming of love, and the realization that life could possibly be better if it was shared with the right person. I certainly do. I clearly remember the evening I met Rosita in a bar in Mermentau, Louisiana. I was bartending and she came in with her girlfriends.

Rosita was an attractive, brown-haired woman with deep green eyes. She was feisty in spirit. Besides her good looks, she was so accepting of me. I came to understand what unconditional love really meant. She was dating someone else, but, luckily, she found me attractive. It was 1981, a year that was to finally end my many years of running. However, it was not the year that I would stop hiding from the dark reality of my yesterdays.

I had so little to call my own. I basically had two sets of clothes, a car with a busted headlight, and baggage that included a lifetime of running away to escape an irreconcilable past. But Rosita immediately saw value in me. She described me to her friends as a quiet, nice, and handsome drifter. These words were welcoming to me. They described someone who was at least better than the person that I had become or thought I had become after many years of decadent living.

I was dating another woman from the area, but I broke up with her to date Rosita. After all, Rosita was the first woman who found something of worth in me. She was not afraid to tell me how she felt or what she was thinking. She thrilled me and frightened me at the same time. When I finally told her my story and she shared it with her friends, she was told to run as far away from me as she possibly could. She was also warned that I would make her an old woman with all the trouble I carried within me. These remarks scared me because I had not told Rosita everything about me. Sure, I told her about the murders, my brother's part in the crime, and bits and pieces of my marriages. There were so many layers of emotional scars that I could not have possibly explained them to her.

Rosita knew there was something more to me, something that she was willing to take the time and energy to discover. She felt sorry for me and for all the pain I had lived through. Poor thing, she did not realize the many things that I was to continue to hide from her. I feared she just could not possibly love me if she knew everything about me. Yet, she remained steadfast in her efforts to bring out the good in me and she kept telling me that she thought she could possibly fall in love with me. She was perceptive enough to know something was still troubling me. She knew that I was holding much of my pain inside. She never feared that I might be a bad person like my brother. She just believed in me. Her belief in me scared me. It was also what saved me.

In the beginning of our relationship, we tried living together. She had a job and was a dependable employee. I was not motivated and continually could not find substantial work. She went to work every day and I stayed home totally unmotivated to find work. Finally, after about eighteen months, she told me: *"Dave, things have to change. I cannot continue to live unmarried in the same house with a man that refuses to obtain and keep a job."* I was so afraid of failing at another relationship. My fear caused me to run again. I left the relationship for a period of time.

We both missed each other and would see each other from time to time. It was not long before I went to Rosita and humbly declared my love for her. I asked her to marry me, and she agreed. I sought out a job and made up my mind that I was going to work so that this relationship would be different from my past relationships. I would live decently, support my spouse both financially and emotionally and finally find happiness. I worked at obtaining a divorce from my third wife.

We got married in Jennings, Louisiana, on August 19, 1984, in a simple ceremony performed in her home by a justice of the peace. We wanted a simple wedding. We wore blue suits, served cake and punch, and united our lives together on that bright and sunny day in August. Her children were present to witness the union. The only somewhat sentimental thing that happened after the brief ceremony was that I looked over at Rosita and stated, *"Hope you know I love you. I married you."* While this sentence is far from some gushing, romantic sonnet, I realized that by pledging my life to this woman I was making a sincere effort to not make the same mistakes in this relationship, and to work toward living a decent married life.

In time, it has been her love and acceptance of me that has virtually taught me how to live. It has been the journey that I share with Rosita that taught me stability in life and stability in love. Our life together is relatively peaceful. Nothing is spectacular about our life. We have had our ups and downs. We have lived in a variety of places, purchasing or renting. We remain in Jennings because it is a peaceful town, a town that allows me to remain fairly unnoticed. Rosita was eventually able to quit working. I have done my best to support her. We live modestly, but happily.

Rosita knows that there is a richer depth that has not been reached in our relationship. She continually tells me that I still have not fully grieved enough or in the proper ways. I wonder what she means by all of that. If she means that I still wonder how my brother could have been involved in such a hideous crime, she is correct. I find it hard to let it go from my thoughts. If she means that I still wonder if life would have been any different if I had not purchased what I thought was to be a hunting gun, she is correct in that I do grieve for that. She tells me that my grief stifles me at times, making me sad, and making me closed to the outside world, including her. She does often find me in very deep thought.

You see, when she met me I was part of a masquerade. I kept trying to be the happy-go-lucky bachelor. It was all a facade. I reflect on the personality I developed so that I could maintain friends and find a family. It was not the person I was emotionally. My inner turmoil continued due to this fact. Who was I?

As our years together have grown in number, she continues to be my best friend, but she does not truly and fully know all she needs to know about me. I know she continues to wait patiently for my healing. She always tells me that she knows there is more bothering me. She wants me to talk to her. I have tried, but there is still so much confusion and shame.

Rosita encouraged me to find someone to help me tell my story. She thinks that by telling my story I will be released from the torment I have held locked within my mind, heart, and soul for years. If in fact there can be healing by reliving this story within the pages of this book, then I needed to do just that. I know that Rosita often feels rejected and alone. She does not deserve to feel that way. I want so much to change that. I want to be the man that she still believes lies beneath the surface. I want to be what she needs me to be for her. She told me recently that she hopes this book will tear down the walls of fear and doubt. She hopes that I will become a man who gives to life and enjoys life to the fullest. It is so simple a wish, but I fight my prison sentence.

Chapter Sixteen
My Quest For Peace

As I mentioned earlier, it was in 2005 that I finally stopped running from my emotions and decided that I had to deal with reality. I knew that to stop the madness of my continual cowardice, I had to return to Kansas and face the very people I had spent a lifetime running from. Living on a limited budget makes traveling difficult. Rosita and I saved money and then borrowed some from a life insurance policy to afford the trip to Kansas. My wife's daughter, Roberta, came with us to assist in driving the 960 miles from Jennings, Louisiana, to Kansas City.

We left at 6 am one hot August morning and arrived in Kansas City at 4:30 pm the following day. It was a long trip back to a far removed place and time. My anxiety increased as we neared our destination. How could a lifetime pass so quickly and how could I still have so many unresolved issues to face as an older man? I was nervous and filled with much anxiety about going home. Mentally, I continued to ask myself tons of questions. Would I find my children? Would anyone want to see me or even speak to me? Could I possibly find my parents' graves or my old home place?

My only real contact at this time was Dick's first wife, Carol. Upon our arrival at Carol's home, we were met with the warmest of hearts and the most sincere hospitality. She was gracious in everything she did to make us feel like family. She allowed Rosita an opportunity to know more about my family by showing her old family photos. Up until this point, Rosita had not seen any photos of my parents. Carol also invited her three sons (Dick's sons) to share a meal with us. It was an evening I will cherish to the end of my days.

I kept thinking … these people are my family. I had not had any contact in such a long time. I thought I would feel like a foreigner in a strange land. That was not the case. I was most comfortable with my brother's children. It gave me a part of him to see and touch. I kept swallowing a lump in my throat. My family … my own family really existed.

It is extremely difficult for me to verbalize all of the feelings that overwhelmed me on that evening. After the many years of running away from family and thinking that they all must hate me, it was incredible to be treated so nicely. I kept thinking that I did not deserve to be treated with such kindness and hospitality. One can only imagine how it felt to see Dick's sons, now grown into adulthood. I wanted to know as much as I could know about them in that short visit. I could easily see Dick's features and personality within each of them. These adult nephews now had children of their own. It was another time in which I realized that I had purposely missed so much.

Dick's boys were fortunate in that Carol married a Christian man. Their strong faith life bonded them tightly together. They lived their lives as Christians, and it was very apparent on that evening that they accepted me with no mention of what a coward I was. No mention was ever made as to why I had not been in contact. Acceptance, peaceful acceptance, was the greatest gift they could have offered.

The next day Carol took us to visit my parents' graves. As I became overwrought with guilt, it was Carol who held me in her arms. My tears flowed freely. Standing beside the graves, I could not remember when it was that I had last seen my mom. It seemed that I must have seen her around 1970 or 1971. I did talk with her on the phone around 1977 or 1978. What a terrible record of communication for the last remaining child of a pitiful and grieving widow. My shame was piercing! I was overcome with remorse and self-condemnation for not having been back to see her before she died. What kind of son was I? I felt sick to my stomach and light-headed.

My grief was indicative of all that had happened to my parents, for all that I had done to my parents, and for all that I had not done for my parents. Looking down at their graves, I still had some of the same feelings of many years ago. What if I could change all of this? I felt that same urge to just run as far away as I possibly could, but this time I did not run. Being in my late sixties, I knew this visit to my parents' graves might be my last one. I mustered up enough strength to say my final good-byes.

How I wanted to scream! I did scream inside. My inner voice was screaming, "*Mom and Dad forgive me for anything that I did to add more pain to your aching hearts. Forgive me for not being smart enough to share my feelings. Forgive me for not knowing the proper things to do to get us healed of the painful trauma we experienced. Forgive me for running away like a coward. Forgive me for buying the gun. Forgive me. Forgive me.*"

Carol once again ministered to me with her words and her wisdom. She said, "*Dick, I kept in touch with your mother over the years. She did shed a million tears for you. She prayed constantly for you and for a forgiving heart. Her journey was treacherous at times, but she did obtain a peaceful forgiving heart. Your mom would have welcomed you with open arms no matter when you would have returned.*"

I kept thinking as she spoke that this could not possibly be true. How does a mother forgive so easily? I could not forgive myself. Carol continued speaking about my mom.

"*Your mom walked a close walk with the Lord. She kept trying to smile through the rest of her life. She never complained. She was humble and thankful for whatever she was able to enjoy in her life. You know that it was the example of her life and her prayers that eventually brought your father to accept the Lord into his life before he died.*" I was thankful because I did not know that detail of my parents' life.

All of these stories made me realize that there were indeed powers far greater than mine which had taken care of my parents, and as I walked away from that lonely, yet beautiful site, I remember looking back and thinking an entire lifetime had passed. I was an old man. I wondered how much time I had remaining in my life to correct my awful mistakes? It was too late for my dear mom, but would it be too late for my daughters and my son? Would I ever be able to find my daughters and talk with them face-to-face?

Our visit continued over the next few days. We spent time seeing Kansas, sharing meals, and talking. Talking with Carol about the past allowed me to share with someone that was as close to the crime as I was. She had stayed the course. She had raised Dick's sons. She had been a devout Christian. She had followed a process in her life for healing. She attributed her courage to the Lord. I remember thinking that I had not done any of the things she had done to help myself move on with my life in a positive or spiritual way. Sure, I went to church, but I never felt any miraculous cure from my memories.

Carol continued in her calm way of guiding my thoughts: *"Dave, our Lord is a forgiving Lord. You must come to forgive yourself. This tragedy affected all of our lives. I quickly realized after Dick's car accident there were very apparent changes in his personality. He looked differently and acted very differently from the person he was before the accident. His looks, of course, had changed, but it was his behavior that had people talking. Even after the murders and I read accounts about Dick I had to wonder of whom the reporters were speaking. The Dick of whom they wrote and spoke about was no one I had ever known.*

"It was at this time that I began to wonder if Dick had another personality, one that developed as a result of the trauma to his head during the accident. I even wondered if his brain had been damaged because he was an automobile painter and had inhaled so many fumes. You know, Dave, in those days, there were no regulations enforced about wearing protective clothing and masks when working in that profession. One thing I was certain of was that Dick Hickock had a change in personality. I often pondered about that radical change and whether it was the reason for his unexplainable behavior on the night of November 15, 1959."

I was amazed at this woman who had shared in the drama and had become a stronger, reflective person. Unlike me, Carol made time for herself and her children to grieve. She talked more of her life after the execution.

"Dave, I waited until school was out for the summer, and then planned a trip to the cemetery. That first visit to the cemetery to bring flowers is etched into my mind. I just had the two oldest boys and my simple intention was to allow them to pay tribute to their father. There were two reporters at the grave when I arrived. The chaplain that had accompanied me on my visit to the grave asked the reporters to please not take pictures. I was trying to shield the boys from the press and from any additional publicity about the crime.

"Both reporters promised not to publish a story about our visit. However, a few days later I read an article in a newspaper that reported the fact that Dick Hickock's first wife visited his grave to lay flowers. I was furious and hurt, but it was about this time that I realized it would be a long time before Kansas and the United States would stop talking about the Clutter murders.

"Once, when I was sitting in a doctor's office, the murders became the topic of discussion. A lady I had never seen or met before began discussing the murders and mentioned that she was an intimate friend of Carol Hickock. I sat dumbfounded as I stared at a woman whom I had never laid eyes on before claimed a part in the notoriety.

"I knew at that moment that I must maintain a low profile, especially for the sake of my three boys. I made a commitment to myself to keep my children's lives as private as was humanly possible. This was a primary reason when I was approached about writing my own book to describe my life with Dick Hickock that I declined. I saw no point in telling my intimate stories to a world that only wanted to know of the despicable details. I wanted my boys to remember the beauty and gentleness of their father."

It was sad for Carol and for many of us when we read FBI accounts of the murder or when we read *In Cold Blood*. All the accounts seemed to speak of a Dick Hickock we did not know. He was a meticulous and caring individual, but he was portrayed as slovenly, arrogant, and coldhearted. Carol knows that now that the boys are older they can reflect on what good memories they have in their minds. Sadly, the youngest son has no memories, except of his experiences in coming to terms with a man he never knew but who was his biological father.

One aspect of Carol's life that assisted her in providing stability for her sons was her second husband. He was a self-assured man who encouraged Carol with her sons and eventually adopted them. Only the two older boys fully understood the seriousness of their biological father's actions. Carol had not wanted her youngest son to ever find out who his real father was, but he ended up finding out in an unfortunate way. Carol thought that since he never knew anyone but her new husband as his father, she would not need to mention the truth. This decision came back to haunt Carol many years later.

Carol was working as an executive housekeeper at a local hotel when she received a call from the school counselor regarding her youngest son. He was in junior high school and the English class topic of the day was the book *In Cold Blood*. He became very upset as he looked at a picture of the murderer Dick Hickock. He had some sort of instant recognition and in his heart he knew that this man was his father. Carol thinks he made the connection because she had never ceased communication with my mom. In fact, she visited often and had a key to their home. The boys called her Grandma Hickock.

When Carol realized that her son had tied the pieces of the story together, she knew she had waited much too long to tell him the truth. She brought her son back to the hotel with her and called Jim Post, a chaplain from the Kansas State Penitentiary. He went to the hotel to talk with the young boy. Mr. Post tried to explain the situation in which Dick Hickock had found himself, the kind of behavior he exhibited while in prison, and his bravery when facing his execution. Carol then scheduled another visit to the cemetery.

On that particular visit, the headstones for Dick Hickock and Perry Smith had been stolen. Thrill seekers were always visiting the graves and Carol guessed one of them had taken the headstones as souvenirs. All these many years later and still the graves of these two men inspire fascination among strangers. Carol took the boys each year to put flowers on their father's grave. The boys continued this practice even after they became old enough to drive. Carol believed that the tradition was cathartic for the boys in their search for healing from their grief.

Looking back on the family's experiences after the murders and Dick's execution, Carol shared her thoughts on the trauma that her two older boys suffered.

"Right after the arrest, a teacher from the elementary school contacted me to inform me of an incident in which she found my second son crying on the steps of the school. When he was asked what the problem was, he openly said, 'I think they are going to kill my dad.' I can only imagine the hurt and pain the boys experienced. They only knew a good father who rocked them when they were small, was carefree enough to romp with them, and made them laugh. How could they possibly understand how their father could be a murderer or that an execution by hanging was their father's fate?"

It was during these most difficult periods that Carol considered moving. The boys' principal promised he would do everything in his power to protect the boys from ridicule. He assured her that he knew how children could be callous and cruel, but he would personally counsel the boys.

Carol has stated that the ordeal was the hardest on her youngest son. As he began to learn about his biological father, he believed everything he heard or read about the murders. He was frightened and confused as to why his mother had ever married such a man as Dick Hickock. He questioned her on every aspect of his father and his behavior. Finally, Carol told her son: *"You have to believe that the Dick Hickock I married was a good and honest man. He had many good parts to his personality. I believe you inherited only the very best parts of your father's personality. During the five years of marriage to your dad, he never was in any type of trouble whatsoever."*

It took many conversations and much prayer to assist Carol's youngest son in understanding a man he never knew. She desperately wanted him to come to a realization about the man who was both his father and a notorious criminal. I can only feel pride in the way my former sister-in-law handled such a delicate situation. She was so much braver than I. She did not run; she stayed the course. I am proud to know her. I am proud of her fine sons and their families. My time with them was much too short, but it was heart-warming. I, too, could see the good parts of Dick being displayed in their actions with their families and their interactions with me. I am so humbled by their goodness and their sincerity.

I held onto every word that Carol shared with me about my mom. Carol remained close to her even after the divorce, and Carol commented that my mom maintained a positive relationship with my first wife after I deserted her. It is so strange for me to realize today that my mom had more sense and a greater level of compassion than I did. She did not run away as I had done.

It became important to me to know every detail I could about Mom in those years that I was absent from her life. My heart was gladdened when I realized that she was genuinely happy when Carol found a Christian man to marry. She was proud to have a new son-in-law, even though Carol was not her biological daughter. She had relationships with Dick's sons, something I had neglected to do. I ran from the reality of the crime, and the hurt and pain it inflicted on my life. Never did I realize how I might have been a source of strength for my nephews.

An important story Carol shared with me was that she went to see my mom the night before she died. When my mom was told that there was someone there to see her, she quickly asked, "Is it Dick?" She died the next morning.

I guess I could question why she did not ask about me. After all, Dick was dead and had been dead for a number of years. Yet, when I heard of her last words, I knew why. I once again was reminded that Dick was her favorite. Of course, she loved me, but Dick had that magnetic personality and easygoing spirit, and he was loved by all. He had been the apple of her eye, despite how his life ended. I do not feel jealous that on her deathbed she asked about Dick. I do feel remorseful for having been the scoundrel of a son who ran away. I could have tried to replace Dick. I could have shared my life with her. No, instead I ran.

Once again, I felt pain deep within my heart and soul. I suppose others who realize in life that some mistakes can never be undone are left with similar feelings. I have learned that my choices made other lives very sad. It is one of my life's most painful lessons. I have been left with a regret that cripples my mind and spirit. I continually pray for forgiveness.

Carol gave me something during those short and memory-filled summer days in Kansas. It was something that I did not even know I needed. She gave me powerful words of wisdom. *"Dave, you must go on with your life. You must forgive yourself. I knew your mom quite well. She would not want you to continue in this negative thinking. It has been long enough, much too long. Your mom understood that your running was your way of coping."*

In her gentle and quiet way, Carol gave me words that I think about often these days. She was gentle and calm, but my heart was ravaged and my mind was completely boggled with any notion of forgiveness. My soul became even more tortured.

As time has passed, I realized she gave me permission to rid myself of my unworthiness and turn my regret over to the Lord. Now, all of this might sound very easy to do. Just remember that I had spent forty plus years running scared, suppressing memories, rationalizing events, and believing that I was a nothing. Somehow, I believed to the very core of my being that I was to blame for not being able to make things right. Carol planted seeds that led toward my healing. As wrong as my running was in the scope of all these years, there was nothing more to do than forgive and move on.

I am not a guru on the psychology of the human mind. I do not know theories of brain functions. I am an ordinary man, but I have learned some extraordinary things these past years while writing my story. I work daily to forgive myself. I think that I am beginning to believe that I can be forgiven. I know that I must make peace with myself, with other people, and with my surroundings before I die.

I think that all of this is a process that begins with baby steps. I am beginning to see a clearer picture of the things that happened to me and to my family so many years ago. I began to understand as I listened to Carol's stories. Every person affected by the crime had to find his or her own way to deal with the pain and the confusion it brought into their lives. Brave and courageous people like Carol give me examples of what I should have done. I am trying to use their witness today as I tell my story. Carol tells me that the process is all a part of a bigger plan in another realm. I wish I had her faith, her belief, and her courage. She is an amazing woman.

Chapter Seventeen

Rosita's Experience In Kansas

It was Rosita's many gentle and not so gentle reminders of the obligation I had to my children that prompted me to seek them out and explain to them the burden I had run from those many years ago. It was she that wanted me to return to Kansas. Rosita believed my children needed to know that my running away never set me free. The burden was greatly increased by my cowardice. She knew the depths of my pain.

Approximately four weeks into our relationship back in the 1980s, I began to share bits and pieces of my life with Rosita. I protected myself by not telling her all the details. She felt immense pity for me and probably wanted to rescue me since she knew that I had never previously opened my heart and life to anyone. She knew much about my brother, the infamous Dick Hickock. She knew much less about my other wives and children. I withheld my feelings and thoughts about my other families. In actuality, I kept much secret because it was just too painful to share.

Rosita knows more than anyone else in this world. She admits that she is learning even more as I am writing this story. The time spent reliving the events of my life and in explaining the emotions my decisions have put me through has given my wife insight into the soul of a tortured man. Now she understands why I often hold back my emotions. I fear that if I let my guard down, the emotions that might come out would be those of a madman needing release from my disappointment, fear, regret, and, most importantly, my guilt.

It was Rosita's urgent encouragement that sent us on the expedition to Kansas. She still had doubts about our venture. Her children were a bit frightened for her about finding a family that was scarred by murder. Rosita even thought she must be insane to seek a family that she might find revolting. Instead, she was thankful for the Kansas trip, for as it unfolded she found a beautiful family, an ordinary family. She found a family that survived a tragedy that others can only imagine. Rosita enjoyed the visit with Carol, and commented that it should bring closure for me on my pain.

The emotional visit to my parents' grave was a memorable part of the Kansas trip for me. Rosita shared with me how she felt as she witnessed me standing pitifully at the graves of my parents. As I openly sobbed in Carol's arms, Rosita felt sadness in her heart and she prayed, asking forgiveness for me. She pleaded with God, explaining that I was just a scared young boy with no way of knowing what to do to handle such a huge problem.

I am not a strong believer in supernatural events. I try hard to believe in a Lord that is kind and good. I really do not think that there could be signs for me from another realm. Yet, something happened to Rosita during our visit with Carol that still leaves me puzzled to this day. Rosita has a stronger faith life than I do. I have always admired her for her faith in prayer. It is because of her faith that I think the following phenomenon may have occurred during the night.

Rosita was spending a sleepless night wondering what the final outcome of this visit to my roots would bring into our lives. At one point during the night, Rosita felt a kiss upon her cheek. In a matter of seconds, as she strained in the darkness to see the figure (or shadow), the entire apparition faded. She tried to awaken me, but I did not stir. I had gone to bed emotionally drained and exhausted.

What could be the meaning to such a strange and surreal experience? Rosita thinks my mom's spirit reached out to her in gratitude for taking care of me. When she told me the story, I did not believe her. She insisted that it was not a dream and she insisted that she was fully awake. She believes that it was one of those experiences that come without any expectation or explanation.

As this past year of 2006 has continued to move quickly by and I have had some moments of peace, I sometimes wonder and hope that what Rosita saw was truly the spirit of my mom. Who knows where reality and fantasy intersect? I would so much want to believe that Mom knows I am doing okay. I would want to be assured that she knows I cried tears of shame at her grave, begging for her to forgive me for all that I had done to neglect her. I would want her to know that at this late stage of my life I am seeking to resolve the issues that I ran away from, the issues that kept me locked up inside for many long and lonely years.

When Rosita met and married me, she knew a man who wore a mask. My mask was something I created to be accepted by others. It was my barrier against an unforgiving and cruel world. The mask was that of a fun man, a happy-go-lucky man. I was always jolly, making others laugh, and I was very romantic with Rosita. Over the years, I believe I have disappointed her. In my search for meaning and in my grief, I have changed. My disposition is sullen and often quiet to the point of moroseness. I forget to reach out in loving ways, because I am still obsessed with trying to make sense out of my yesterdays.

Rosita remarked recently that she hopes that by writing my story I will come to understand the peace of the forgiveness of my heavenly Father. She hopes that I can release my tears and my fears, and that I will be able to more openly express myself. If I can do this, she hopes to find the man whom she has lost along the way. I hope, how I hope, that I can do this for her and for me. Maybe my story will be of help to others who have haunting memories. I only hope we can all find peace.

Chapter Eighteen
My Children

I will not tell anyone the names of my children. One thing I failed to do years ago was protect them. I was not present to help them through anything they may have had to face in their lives. When they were teased at school for being a Hickock, I was not there. When they were as afraid and paranoid as I was, I was not there. When they had birthday parties, I was not there. When they celebrated holidays, I was not there. I was a deserter, a neglectful father, and a renegade. When I think of the pain I caused in their lives, I am truly sorry.

As I said earlier, it was at Rosita's urging that I decided to begin searching for my children. At her first insistence that I do so, I continued to shut out her suggestions. I was too insecure to venture into that area. Rosita knew I had a special place in my heart for my children even though I tried to hide my feelings about them from her. She knew I always remembered each child's birthday. When I told Rosita about their approaching birthdays, she encouraged me to try to contact my children. She often begged me to reconsider, advising me that perhaps they wanted to see me. Remembering their birthdays was the only thing I had left of the children I had abandoned.

Then, quite unexpectedly, Rosita answered the phone one warm summer day in 2005 and the young woman calling asked if she had reached the residence of Walter David Hickock. When Rosita verified the fact that she did indeed have the correct residence, the young woman stated that she was one of Walter David Hickock's daughters and that she needed some answers. Rosita thanked her for calling and told her that she would relay the message to me. She quickly drove to Wal-Mart, where I worked, to tell me about the call.

I cannot even begin to explain my feelings on that day. The news made me visibly shake. I do not know if it was just my nerves wreaking havoc or if I was filled with emotions that included anticipation, joy, and fear. I just remember wanting to return home as quickly as I could to return the call. My shift at work seemed to last forever. I kept looking at my watch and anticipating the conversation. I was finally getting a chance to reconnect with one of my children. In my mind I continued to think of what words to say. Would she be happy she found me? Would she be angry with me for what I had done? Would she hate me? I wanted her to just listen and let me explain. Would she allow me that privilege?

With great apprehension, I returned home to call my daughter. She was the child I fathered with my second wife. As I listened to my child, I quickly understood that it was not a child talking to me, but an adult. I was both excited and frightened of the possibilities of what might transpire. My daughter related to me that she recently had troubles in her life and was trying desperately to overcome them and start anew. She seemed eager to tell me all of the details of her difficulties and trying times. I wanted to talk forever with her about all of the many events I had missed. I listened to some of her sad stories about her difficulties, her news of her son, my grandson, and an update on the people she had in her life.

My ears were hearing her words, but my heart was crying out. *"Stop! Stop! I have so much to say to you. It was my fault. Anything that went bad in your life is my fault. I am the reason that you have had so many crosses to bear. It must have been because I abandoned you at such a young age. Your choices were because of me. You used so many other ways in your life to mask the pain of my abandonment. I gave you reason to run from the harshness of reality and find alternatives to the love and acceptance of a father. Your pain is my responsibility."*

My stomach was sick and my head was spinning. I understood once again what it meant to have your heart broken. There was so much to say, but so little I could do to change what I had caused by my abandonment.

I wanted to ask about arranging a visit with her so that I could really discuss her life and mine. I could not muster the courage to do so. That was a mistake. Shortly after our phone conversation, my daughter moved and I was left with no phone number or forwarding address. I do not think she was running away from me. However, I do believe she was probably running away from her life.

I would occasionally call her mother's residence in an effort to locate her. If my daughter was there, she was always willing to speak, but that was never enough for me. Those brief conversations and the long distance between us gave me a desire to see and talk with her. She did make an effort to write to me. She even sent photos. How I treasured those photos! I would often look at them, seeking similarities in faces and comparing those faces with my own or those of my family.

I continued to ask myself questions about how I could have possibly made a change in her attitude, and, consequently in her life, if I had been present as she went through the normal stages of growing into womanhood. I could have told her about the dangers and pitfalls of the bad decisions we make in life. I could have explained to her that it was part of maturing to face the many complexities of life. I wanted to share with her that I knew my neglect was to blame for her problems. I just knew that I was responsible, and once again I felt the same shame and heartache. A phone conversation was such a poor replacement for face-to-face contact, especially after all those years.

I wanted so much to belong to my children and I wanted them to belong to me. To this day, I often wonder if my daughter has managed to stay on a positive road in her life. I pray that she has the courage to do so. I pray that she has been blessed and her emptiness has vanished. I sincerely hope her searching has assisted her in determining a positive approach to her future. Of course, I still carry the cross of blame upon my shoulders for the many sad circumstances of her life. Just maybe I could have helped her more, loved her more, and given her a brighter life.

Another adult daughter, from my first wife, called one day stating that her doctor told her to call me. I did not even ask what doctor or if she was sick. I just listened and was more than willing to talk and answer any questions as truthfully as I possibly could. I remember holding the phone as close to my ear as possible. I guess I thought that would make her real to me. I longed to hold her in my arms.

She relayed to me that she was trying to put together the pieces of her life. One of her first questions was that she wanted to know exactly when I left and never returned. I really had to think about that reply. In my younger days, my jobs provided me with many times of leaving home and then returning. She just wanted to clearly remember the very last time I went to see them and then walked out of their lives forever. As I tried to remember, I was overcome with emotions. I was ashamed that I could not even give her an exact date or even an exact year. I told her it must have been around 1966 or 1967.

My mind reeled with the immensity of what I had done. I held back and remained silent, but I do remember what I wanted to say: "*Not only did I desert our family; I have no memory of when I did such an evil deed. I cannot even remember your ages when I left. It was not that I did not care. Please believe me. I was a scared and confused man.*" I did not share these words because I wanted to share them with her in person. I felt nauseous, my palms were wet, and my heart began to beat wildly.

Why couldn't I have just stated, "I ran away because I was scared and wanted to save my children from embarrassment. I know! I know that I was a coward. I am so sorry. Please, please forgive me." The words just would not come, though my thoughts were racing.

She then shared another tragedy. It was about her brother, my son, who had become very ill. He had wanted her to find me so he could speak to me because he was dying. I held my breath for the next words and then I pleaded with her to tell me where he was and said I would go to him immediately. She paused and then told me in a quiet voice that it was too late. Those words sent a piercing coldness throughout my body. I was not there for my son during his entire life, his illness, and finally his death. My stomach was tight, my heart was beating fast, my head felt light, and my body began to shake. I was so ashamed and now so pained to know that a child of mine had died before I could offer my repentance and beg for forgiveness.

Before my daughter ended the conversation, she did share a good memory of me, a faint but fond memory of my taking her fishing at Garrett Lake. I was so relieved that she had that memory. I had not thought of any of those times. I had possibly suppressed even the good memories. I had drowned myself in all my regret, misery, and self-pity, and I had never once remembered anything of value that I had done with or for my children. I thanked her for sharing that memory with me.

My daughter told me she was looking for closure. I did not really understand what closure was at that moment. Yet, she seemed happy with just making contact with me. I finally told her that I wanted to see her in person to tell her the entirety of the story. I thanked her for calling me, and I told her to call anytime and I would answer every question as honestly as I possibly could. In my nervousness, I failed to get her phone number. The wait to hear from her again would drive me to such panic. We finally did reconnect via the phone and then scheduled a visit to her home. She still calls me every now and then. I am grateful for those calls.

During our trip to Kansas in 2005 we included a visit to one of my daughters, who had called me. Her husband and her son, my grandson, were at home and greeted us. They were cordial and asked if we would like coffee. We sat quietly for a time before my grandson, a very tall, talented, and artistic young man, began making conversation with me. I could not help but search his face to see me in him. I could see myself. That fact alone made me proud and sad at the same time. He shared that he had been responsible for cleaning the house for our visit. He talked of his athletic escapades and the fact that he was a very good basketball player. He wanted to know if I had been good at basketball. I shared a few things about my athletic endeavors.

I kept thinking what a nice young man he was and that he had to have inherited the artistic talent from my former wife, his grandmother. I was also saddened because I had missed so much of his life. I knew that in just a few short minutes I would leave Kansas to return to Louisiana, and, in doing so, I would miss even more of his life. He was my grandchild, my flesh and blood. I had abandoned his mother and now I would abandon him.

When my daughter arrived, she parked outside the house and stayed in her car for a while. My nerves were giving me fits. I was shaking, just knowing that she was hesitant to come into her own home. When she finally came in, she first went and hugged Rosita and then Roberta, Rosita's daughter. She then hugged me. She told me that when she drove up to her driveway and saw Louisiana plates on the car parked there, she knew I had arrived. She cried tears of joy and anticipation as she sat in her car, with conflicting emotions on whether or not to come in the house to meet me. Her tears dried quickly as she pulled out photos and began to talk about the family.

Eventually, the conversation centered on the crime and the book *In Cold Blood*. She had read the book and she disputes some of the so-called facts in it. She had heard many different stories about the crime over the years. She was at a point at which she did not believe all of the details about the crime. She was tired of hearing about the entire ordeal. I sat there trying to find the right words. Even when words came to my mind, they were even more difficult to speak.

I finally told her I was going to find an author to tell the Hickock family's side of the story, my own personal heartbreak associated with the crime, and its drastic affects on our entire family. She agreed that this venture would be an important one. I mentioned that I wanted to have a chance to talk with the other girls, my daughters. I got the impression that they did not want to have anything to do with me.

I just asked her point blank, *"Is there any chance your sisters would want to see me?"*

She replied very compassionately, *"No, they are not ready for that. They have heard such bad things about you through the years. They are not willing to see you."*

I cried.

I knew they did not owe me a thing. I also knew that I must be near them geographically at the exact moment when, or if, they changed their minds and did want to see me. The thought of leaving Kansas without speaking with them left me feeling spiritually disillusioned. It was at this point that my daughter reached out to hug me. She said, *"Dave, I love you. You are, after all, my real dad."*

I immediately knew what she meant. She loved me because I was her biological father. She somehow did need that connection with me. At the same time, I understood that there was a real father in her life and it was not me. The man that had been there for her was much better than all of my dead end attempts of running scared. I was glad she had him. I was fortunate that she showed some kindness to me. She and her family walked us to our car.

That visit ended in a pleasant and friendly manner. My heart and mind, however, felt anything but pleasant. I was relieved to have met her. I was saddened by the truth that my chances of connecting with my other children were running out. I just wanted to say a few words to them. I wanted the chance that I had just experienced with this particular daughter on this summer evening. I never wanted to interfere with their lives in a negative way. I just wanted them to know the truth about me. I wanted them to understand that I definitely know what I did, how grave a misdeed it was, and that I was deeply and sincerely sorry.

I have learned that loving from a distance leaves so much to be desired. Even as I understand the miracle of sorts I was able to enjoy with that one daughter, I am left with a deep desire to find all my children. It is something that I will continue to long for until the day I die.

I am getting older. My wish is that I live long enough to complete this book, and that my children will read it. My children consisted of three daughters and one son from my first marriage. My second marriage included one son and one daughter. I had no children with my third wife, as we were married for a short while.

I want my children to know and understand the message within the pages of this story. I want them to know that I understand exactly how horrible my deeds of neglect to them were. I am open to hear what they have to say. I stand ready to beg for forgiveness. I do not expect to become their most adored and long-lost father. I realize that there were good men who became their fathers. Those men were man enough to do something that I chose not to do. For their dedication in raising my children, I stand in sincere gratitude. Their places of honor at my children's sides are well earned and most deserved. I just want time to make peace.

Chapter Nineteen
Message To My Children

When a person gets to be my age, time and regret can almost cripple one's thoughts. I am not a well man. I am no longer the man that could climb water towers with agility and skill. I am older now, fighting arthritis and a variety of other health issues. Often these days, I wonder how much time I have left. I do not want pity from anyone. I just want to complete my story. I keep trying to fill in the blanks. Even as I have reflected and my life story is coming together on the pages of this book, I feel so lonely. One might say, *"The old man deserves to be lonely. Think of what he did in running away all these years."* Those statements are absolutely true. Yet, how can I complete my story on earth? Could I or will I ever make a reunion happen for my children and me?

If today was to be my last day on this earth, I wonder what my last request would be. I can hardly speak as my heart breaks for my children. My tears are streaming down my face and I am ashamed. My final request would be to see my children. I want to be brave and not the coward that I have been all these years. I want to share with them that I fully realized that there are many things I could have done differently.

At the time of my cowardly running, I was a young man who became a young adult who actually thought his absence would make everyone's life easier. I want to beg forgiveness for what I put my mom, my wives, and my children through. None of the events, none of my behavior, and none of the notoriety was their fault. They were innocent victims of my uncaring and unjust ways. I can only imagine the loneliness they experienced because of my actions. My loneliness today has to pale in comparison to their entire lives coping with my neglect of them.

I want my children to know that my running did not mean I did not love them or think of them almost every day of my life. I want them to understand how many times I wanted to go back to Kansas to find them. I want them to know that I realize they suffered so much, and that much of their suffering was due to my insensitivity and cowardice. Yes, it was my fault. I take all of the blame!

I know that I am asking for something I do not deserve. Deep down within my being I do not believe I deserve anything from them. This fact alone has kept us separated for a lifetime. I often think of what words to use to make my children understand the pain, regret, and remorse in my heart. I think that asking them to accept what I did is asking way too much. In reality, it is too late to expect that. Why would they forgive me?

A father leaving home is a terrible thing to do to children. I punished all of them as well as myself by not being present to witness their various stages of growing up. I have only a few pleasant memories of my children. I remember the love I felt for them when they were born. Once reminded, I did remember the fishing trips with them to the lake. My memories, however, as an old expression I heard long ago states, are *a whole lot of little much too late.* You see, I have no memories of them taking their first steps, celebrating their birthdays, the excitement of their first dates, their difficulties in school or life, or any such normal activities. My slate is clean, empty. The position I should have held as their father is also empty on their slates.

If I could have a perfect world, I would take away any feeling they have experienced of abandonment and I would hold them in my arms and tell them that everything I did was wrong. I would tell them that it is very difficult for me to forgive myself, so I would understand why forgiveness would not be easy for them.

To make matters even more difficult, I heard last summer that one of my daughters was very ill. Knowing that and not being able to help her in any way worries me. I even wonder if the life she lived in which I was absent caused her so much stress that she developed a serious illness. Could that be another terrible thing to add to my accomplishments in life? I cry out in sadness because I fear that no one, including my children, would believe me!

I am not going to stop my efforts to find my children. They will always be close to my heart. They may or may not read this book. Yet, at least I can be thankful that if they do, they will know that in my final days I had to come to terms with the scoundrel that I am. They will have to know that even a scoundrel can have love and concern in his heart for his children.

In the time I have remaining on this earth, I pray for blessings. For what? I need help to be relieved from my guilt … to be freed from my shame … to be reminded that even though I purchased the gun used as a murder weapon I am not the one who masterminded a plan for murder. I long to be released from the regret of neglecting my mother and abandoning my children. I may have only a short "tomorrow" left … I just want peace. I am looking to heavenly powers for the healing, mercy, and blessings of a peaceful life free of sorrow and pain.

Chapter Twenty
Quiet Days On End

I continue my work as a greeter for Wal-Mart. The focus on the Clutter murders does not plague me as it once did. A local newspaper did a few articles on my connection to the crime as a Hickock. Now that people of this area have read the articles, I am occasionally asked if I am the one related to the murderer. I shudder as I hear those words today.

I guess that people have watched so many crime shows and murder mysteries that they are calloused to the pain that murder can bring a family. I find it hard to believe that people can be so cold. And yet, if I put their questions into perspective, the people asking me about the crime today are much kinder than any of the ones who hurt my mom and dad with their vicious calls and their blatant ostracism in Kansas so many years ago. Some tell me they feel sorry for me and for the pain life caused me. Some tell me that they can tell that I am a good person and that they understand how my life must have been quite difficult. Many have encouraged me to tell my story to the world, which I am doing.

I look back and I know I made my life more difficult than it had to be. The cowardly way I ran from the mention of the Hickock name was the most despicable of all my deeds. I hated my name. Strange as it may seem, though, I never hated my brother. I still believe that he was a bit deranged after his accident. I think of how his left eye sank into his face after the accident. I think of how little time was spent with trained individuals who could have determined if my brother was mentally unstable. I wonder if he were alive today and had the advantage of top-notch psychiatrists, whether he would be proven mentally unstable. I think the answer would be a loud and convincing *yes*!

No one in today's world could say and do such strange things without being psychologically evaluated. I hear about people involved in less violent crimes who were furnished with all types of evaluations. I wish my brother had had an opportunity to receive a conscientious evaluation of his mental state. Then perhaps I would have been able to understand why he chose to drive 400 miles across Kansas to the small town of Holcomb to participate in committing murder!

I may sound like I continue to drag up old news, the past and all its pain. I want you to know that by finally telling my story I am trying to determine what my own purpose in this drama has been. I am trying to determine my own purpose in life. I try hard to balance the wonderful memories I have of my parents, the farm, and the good times shared with family and friends while growing up with the pain that began with Dick's involvement in the Clutter murders. I spend much time now talking to the Lord, for I am told he will bring me to an understanding of why I am still around trying to make sense of my life.

My parents gave us a strong foundation for life. They taught us right from wrong. They tried to provide all we needed to grow into adulthood: an education, home, nutritious meals, and some spiritual background. I cannot say my brother and I were deprived of anything. We had the basics and much security.

In trying to solidify my thoughts, I am making an effort to put all the events into some order for me and for my family. My family was never the same after the crime. We never were able to iron things out. I never stayed around anywhere long enough to do that. I never was able to be true blue to anyone except possibly Rosita. In looking over my life, I can finally ask forgiveness from the people I hurt the most. My biggest battlefield still remains inside my own head.

It has taken me a long time to work out the events of my life and finally put them into perspective. The truth is it has taken me an entire lifetime. But the many years of trying to understand and make sense of all of the events have given me opportunities to grieve, to reflect, and to face my faults. I still often believe that my life can only make sense if I face the future with courage as I try to undo my mistakes.

Even though the most pressing events happened years ago, I am hoping that by writing this book I can help someone. I read in the newspaper and hear on news broadcasts about all sorts of evil doings in today's world. Perhaps my story will provide those who must face traumatic events an opportunity to learn from my many mistakes. My plea is that anyone in similar situations should definitely not do things in the way that I did. I urge them to reach out for professional assistance, stand by their families, and face fears head on! I also stress to never forget that God has healing for us. We must believe in his healing power.

It appears that I will have to work very hard to find my other children. I know the general area where they might be living. You would think it would be easy in this day of computers to locate people, but I do not even know the married names of my daughters. My plan is that when I find them I will not interfere with their lives in any manner. Part two of my plan is that once I find my children, I am going to be as honest and open as I possibly can. I just want one chance to explain to them face to face.

Even as I try to verbalize what I did, I know that everything I try to write or say seems to be just another excuse. The truth is I am a coward who ran away from everything that mattered to me. My mind and body were turned in the wrong direction. Even if my children do not understand, I want the chance to beg forgiveness. I know there cannot be any making up of lost time. I swallow a hard lump in my throat when I think of what a pity that is. I just want them to know that I have loved and missed them all of my life. I want them to have a copy of my book. I am sorry that this book will not fill in all the blanks, but I am hoping and praying it may be a source of insight.

Epilogue

I don't need anyone to feel sorry for me. Why? Because I have done enough of that on my own. I want my story told to make sure that anyone who happens to be in a situation similar to the one I found myself in during that fateful year of 1959 and beyond can learn something from my story. I urge those of you with heartaches to go beyond your reality, your trauma, and find help. That help could be medical or psychological attention, within the walls of your church, or by finally finding a way to tell your story. At this point, just telling my story is providing a release of sorts. I talk more about every detail as my biographer makes me dig really deep within myself for the emotions I felt at various times of my life. They are coming forth like an unending waterfall. I had them locked away for so very long, I never thought I had so much to say. These words are releasing some of my pent-up emotions. Now, when I ask God for help, I know what I am asking. I do not just want to forget and live happily ever after. I want to be forgiven.

Afterword

My time with Walter David Hickock will remain a part of my life that has deeply changed the way I look at people. He shared his story as he remembered the details, the relationships, the conversations, and the confusing emotions of a lifetime. His reality was very harsh. People all around us suffer from the realities of life, harsh realities of varying depths.

When I hear the latest news about some incredibly sad situation, I think compassionately about the family that must deal with the embarrassment and pain inflicted on them by a member of their own family. I lament that not all people know of a forgiving Lord and Savior. For in our most troubled times and in our most disappointing of circumstances, the only real answer lies in the belief in a power that is greater than any evil that can occur in our world.

I wish that Walter David Hickock had an understanding of such a Lord when he was left to deal with the murders and the turmoil that followed him during the remainder of his life. He came to understand during the process of writing this book that forgiveness was the key to moving on in life. I believe that in the interviews and conversations he shared with me, the gentle spirit of a man who had been tortured was beginning to find peace, both within himself and with his Lord. I believe he told his stories with sincerity and with as much truthfulness as he possibly could. I also believe that he was genuinely sorry for the neglect and injury he inflicted on the women and children in his life.

I close my eyes to remember the gentle beauty of his blue eyes and his soft voice, and I wish that once more I could just talk with him and reassure him that peace is what the Lord wants for all of us during and after our trials. Then again, I believe he has indeed found that peace.

Made in the USA
Middletown, DE
24 November 2017